ACCIDENTS IN NORTH AMERICAN MOUNTAINEERING

VOLUME 7 • NUMBER 2 • ISSUE 50

1997

THE AMERICAN ALPINE CLUB
GOLDEN

THE ALPINE CLUB OF CANADA
BANFF

ISSN 0065-082X

ISBN 0-930-410-66-1

Manufactured in the United States of America

Published by
The American Alpine Club, Inc.
710 Tenth Street, Suite 100
Golden, CO 80401

Cover Illustration
Joe LaBelle is featured as the small figure in the foreground on the Klutlan Glacier around 9,000 feet, sprinting out ahead of an avalanche that had released and fallen some 3,000 feet off the West Face of Mount Tressider (13,315'). On the right side of the glacier would be Mount Bona (16,240').

Do avalanches ever go in the same place twice in a short period of time? Yes! On a regular basis. This party—part of the Mount Logan Project—included LaBelle, A.J. LaFleur and Rick Wilcox, who were going up the glacier on avalanche debris, thinking, "If there is this much debris, the slopes above must be stable!" LaBelle wrote it up in *AAJ* as "a close one!" Photograph by Richard French (Rick) Wilcox.

CONTENTS

SAFETY COMMITTEES 1996

The American Alpine Club

John Dill, George Hurley, Jeff Sheetz, Fred Stanley, James Yester,
and John E. (Jed) Williamson *(Chairman)*

The Alpine Club of Canada

Helmut Microys, Orvel Miskiw, Frank Pianka, Paul Ritzema,
Michael Swanguard, Harvey Struss and Murray Toft *(Chairman)*

ACCIDENTS IN
NORTH AMERICAN MOUNTAINEERING

Fiftieth Annual Report of the
Safety Committee of The American Alpine Club

Canada: As of publication date, data and narratives from Canada were not available for this year's report.

United States: This issue marks a half century of the Report of the Safety Committee of the American Alpine Club. The Club constituted a Safety Committee in 1947 by the action of then AAC President, Walter Wood, and it was chaired by William P. House. The other members were M.Beckett Howarth, Maynard M. Miller and David Robertson, Jr. The reason for its formation was due to "the startling increase in the number of mountaineering accidents which occurred" during that summer. The introduction to the 1948 publication *Mountaineering Safety* stated that the purpose of the Safety Committee would be "to investigate climbing accidents and to formulate a program of prevention for the future." They also commented that data was to be gathered "with no intent to criticize persons involved, but rather to learn why these accidents occurred and to emphasize the lessons to be learned from them."

In 1949, the Committee called the 20 page report, printed in the American Alpine Journal, *Safety in the Mountains*. It was compiled and written by Maynard Miller. The committee had added Richard Leonard, Ome Daiber, and Dr. Benjamin G. Ferris, Jr. The next year the report was again printed as a pamphlet and called *Safety and the Climber*. This was followed in 1951 by the title *Alpine Accidents*, in which there was initiated the tabulation of accidents and their statistical information for the previous four years. Hassler Whitney (who took Howarth's place), John Fralick, and Dr. Hans Kraus were added to the committee. There was also an attempt that year to present the number of potential climbers in the U.S. based on membership lists from related organizations. The total of 40,000, which included the Appalachian Mountain Club and the Sierra Club, clearly represented a significant number of hikers. But it was proof enough for the Safety Committee that "more active missionary work by individuals in local clubs" was needed to lure the inexperienced, unprepared, and unjustifiably overconfident into programs of indoctrination.

By 1952, the pamphlet, still at 25 pages, took on its current (almost) name, *Accidents in American Mountaineering*, and tabulations of the 66 mountaineering accidents reported in the United States and Canada for the five year period 1947-1951 were included. Many of the incidents would be considered hiking or scrambling (off trail) situations, not technically to be counted as a mishap in the sport of climbing/mountaineering.

A number of other interesting documentaries and publications came out during this time period. The famous commentator Lowell Thomas narrated a U.S. Forest Service film entitled "Avalanches to Order" in 1949. The Seattle Mountain Rescue Council came out with *Mountain Safety Tips* in the same year. The Colorado Mountain Club published a series of accounts called, "It Can't Happen To Me - But It Did!" A twenty cent booklet by Wolf Bauer of the Seattle Mountain Rescue Council came out in 1952. It was called *You Can Handle an Emergency.*

The report stimulated the development of the Mountain Rescue Association. This group was particularly active in the Western States, and was spearheaded by Peter Shoening and George Sainsbury. They also launched a project to coordinate mountain safety education and rescue, and presented their scheme at the 1958 Annual Meeting of the AAC. Out of this came nine flyers "to provide basic information to climbers throughout North America interested in organizing mountain rescue teams." These were developed by the MRA and published by the AAC.

The format for reporting incidents was established by Dr. Thomas O. Nevison and Dr. Benjamin Ferris, Jr, who in 1952 became the Chairman of the Safety Committee and editor of the report until 1973. He recognized some of the inherent flaws in the Cause and Contributory Cause categories. We know there can be more than one cause for an accident, and that sometimes an "immediate cause," such as falling, is not the underlying cause, such as "exceeding abilities," or "having an off day." Ferris also recognized that it would never be possible to draw statistical conclusions from the data, because not only are they non-parametric, neither can they be looked at linearly. In other words, every accident has at least two or three causes linked with it, but each event is a separate configuration of these. The goal for all the Tables, then, is to illustrate trends. It is useful to know that most fatalities and serious injuries are the result of a fall and/or falling rocks or objects; that they happen only slightly more on ascending than descending; that more often than not it is the inexperienced who get in trouble; and that the young and old are equally afflicted.

A further statistical problem Dr. Ferris tried to overcome was to determine the number of climbers and climber days in any given year. In 1951, outdoor and mountaineering club total membership came to about 40,000, but this number included the Appalachian Mountain Club, Sierra Club, and various similar hiking and trail clubs, totaling 16,000 in all. So the number of people who could be counted strictly as climbers could only be estimated. In 1956, a better tabulation based on two years of figures received from climbing clubs and park registrations was reported. The committee was able to develop risk estimates based on man (sic) mountain days. The mountaineering accident rates were comparable to those in other sports when "standardized" for periods of risk exposure, but the mortalities were higher. However, even these, he recognized, were potentially spurious or misleading. In 1959, more detailed analyses were possible, and the results were presented in graphic form. Additionally, Ferris made an attempt to make some "observations." He noticed that with increasing age the ratio of fatal to nonfatal accidents seems to remain approximately the same. Why? He listed the following possibilities: 1) There is a limit beyond which more experience is of little help in reducing the ratio; 2) with increasing age and more experience more difficult climbs are attempted with more risk involved; and 3) with increasing age physical condition is not maintained, and when an accident occurs even to an experienced climber, he is unable to protect himself adequately.

Dr. Benjamin Ferris, Jr., whose legacy continues in these pages, died in the peaceable kingdom of his home, surrounded by family, in the summer of 1996. This year's edition is dedicated to his memory, with grateful thanks from the current U.S. Managing Editor.

In addition to the Safety Committee, we are grateful to the following individuals for collecting data and helping with the report: Hank Alicandri, Aram Attarian, Micki Canfield, Hal Clifford, Greg Dillman, Ron Cloud, Jim Detterline, Mark Magnuson, Tom McCrumm, Daryl Miller, Russell Peterson, Roger Robinson, Jim Schlinkmann, J. W. Wilder, and, of course, George Sainsbury.

John E. (Jed) Williamson
Managing Editor, USA
7 River Ridge Road
Hanover, NH 03755

Orvel Miskiw
Contributing Editor, Canada
5 Meskanaw Road
RR2 Cochrane
Alberta TOL OWO

UNITED STATES

RAPPEL ERROR—ONLY CONNECTED TO ONE STRAND OF RAPPEL ROPE
Alaska, Anchorage, Hunter Creek

On January 21, Evan Blanchard (20) had climbed to the top of a 150 foot frozen water-fall, and then he and his two partners looped their rope around a tree at the top in preparation for a rappel. The two friends had failed to thread both strands through his rappelling device. With just one end of the rope weighted, he plunged the entire 150 feet, taking the rope with him.

Jeff Sands, a member of the Alaska Mountain Rescue Group, just happened to be walking his dogs and scouting future climbs in the area. He came on the scene ten minutes after the accident.

"He was ugly," Sands said. "There was a lot of blood."

The impact had shattered his helmet, but Sands is sure it saved Blanchard's life. Sands initiated a rescue effort that ended up taking four hours until Blanchard was able to be transferred to a helicopter. (Source: *Anchorage Daily News*, January 22, 1996)

INADEQUATE FOOD AND FUEL, FAILURE TO TURN BACK, INEXPERIENCE
Alaska, Mount Foraker

On April 1, Mitch Ward and Randy Adrian's "Ice Skids" Expedition departed from Talkeetna to the north side of Denali National Park. They were dropped off by K-2 Aviation on a remote frozen lake located north of the Swift Fork River, approximately two miles outside of the Denali Park Wilderness Boundary. Ward and Adrian departed the airstrip for the Northwest Ridge of Mt. Foraker on April 2. They had a P.L.B. for emergencies and approximately 28 days of food and fuel. Their 30 mile approach to the route was shrouded with two to three feet of unconsolidated snow, so it took 14 days.

They started their climb of the Northwest Ridge on April 16, and spent the next nine days climbing to their high camp at 16,400 feet. They were out of food and had less than two days of fuel left. They had been climbing on less calories than they had planned for and decided their situation was bleak. They decided to activate the P.L.B.

At 2135 on April 27, Major Simons from the Alaska Rescue Coordination Center in Anchorage reported that they were receiving a signal coming from the north side of Mt. Foraker. No flights could be launched from Talkeetna that evening due to the inclement weather. The next day, at 1000, Hudson Air, with NPS Ranger Billy Shott aboard, reported that the signal was coming from 16,400 feet on Mt. Foraker. Ranger Shott reported seeing two climbers and one tent. At 1040, the LAMA helicopter was launched from

Talkeetna with Ranger Daryl Miller aboard. They reached the base of Mt. Foraker but weather forced them to land at the 7,200 foot base camp. At 1530, the LAMA launched and flew up along the Sultana Ridge, passing over the two climbers. Both ran out of the tent and immediately started breaking it down. After a radio conference with the Talkeetna Ranger Station, the LAMA lowered a CB radio, park radio, one gallon water, food, and fuel. In about five minutes, Ward called on the park radio requesting a rescue. He stated that they had not eaten in three days and were also severely dehydrated. Ranger Miller instructed Ward and Adrian to hydrate, eat and start their descent as soon as possible. Ward asked which route they should descend. Miller advised that the Southeast Ridge of Mt. Foraker was objectively dangerous due to avalanche activity and recommended the Sultana Ridge. Ward agreed and asked how many days the descent would take. Miller estimated approximately three to five days to the 7,200 foot base camp. Ward and Adrian stayed at their high camp at 16,400 feet for the next four days, deciding that they would rest and hydrate.

On May 3, the "Ice Skids" started their descent. They were spotted at 15,200 feet and contacted by Park Radio via a fixed wing aircraft by Ranger Miller. Ward stated they had two days food and fuel left and were concerned about running out before they reached the 7,200 foot base camp.

On May 4, Mountaineering Ranger Joe Reichert, and volunteers Nina Kemppel and Denny Gignoux departed for Mt. Foraker. They reached 12,000 feet and made camp. The next day, Reichert and Kemppel reached the "Ice Skids" at 1130 in the bowl below peak 12,472. After an hour of eating and drinking the four began their descent to Mt. Crosson. They arrived at camp at 1700. On May 7, all five climbers descended Mt. Crosson and arrived at base camp at 1500. Ward and Adrian flew out to Talkeetna shortly after.

Analysis

The "Ice Skids" team had been briefed extensively in Talkeetna by both an experienced local guide who had previously climbed this route up to 12,000 feet and a mountaineering Ranger who had hiked the approach in the similar time of year. Ward and Adrian were advised that their northern approach to Mt. Foraker could be substantially longer than the time they had allotted. Also, they were warned about their planned food and fuel portions, which were sparse for the typically cold conditions in April. Ward had two climbs into the Alaska Range and Adrian had no experience in Alaska on any climbs. This expedition experienced labor intensive snow conditions on the approach and because of some navigation errors, the approach took 14 days instead of the planned seven. Also, this climb was extremely committing because of the planned traverse, remoteness, length, time of year and no communication.

It would have been prudent to back off the route and return to the landing strip at a much lower elevation than to run out of food and fuel at 16,400 feet. All people traveling into the wilderness areas of Alaska have a personal responsibility to conduct all endeavors based on self sufficiency. (Source: Denali National Park—Talkeetna Subdistrict Ranger Station)

BACK STRAIN
Alaska, Mount McKinley, West Buttress
On May 11, Robert Gray of the "CFS" party twisted his back at the 14,200 foot camp on the West Buttress of Mt. McKinley. Gray's condition deteriorated over the next several days, and by the 13th he could not walk. Their party requested assistance from the

14,200 foot Ranger Station at 1230 on the 13th. On the 14th, two NPS VIP's delivered food, fuel and medicine to the party. Gray improved enough on the 15th to be able to descend without assistance down the mountain, flying out on the 17th.

Analysis
The "CFS" party handled their situation as well as could be expected considering the predicament they were in. A lowering down the rescue gully is a serious matter and should only be conducted in life threatening situations where there are no other options and a helicopter evacuation is not possible. Many complications can arise in this 3000 foot lowering which, once started, cannot be reversed. Waiting for better weather or in this case waiting for the patient to improve so an assisted descent down the ridge could be made is the safest course of action. (Source: Denali National Park - Talkeetna Subdistrict Ranger Station)

AVALANCHE, POOR POSITION
Alaska, Mount Hunter
On May 13, 1996, Marcus von Zitzewitz and Olaf Hecklinger were killed when an avalanche swept them off their climbing route on Mount Hunter.

On May 5, four Germans, Peter Fresia, Franz Perchtold, Marcus von Zitzewitz, and Olaf Hecklinger, flew into base camp on the Kahiltna Glacier. The first objective of the group was the Kennedy-Lowe route on Mt. Hunter. On or around May 5 they abandoned this route because of unsafe snow conditions and objective dangers.

Leaving tents erected at base camp the German group was away from camp on a ski tour for the following five to seven days. Ranger Joe Reichert made his first contact with them at base camp on May 11. On this day the four were busy helping Anne Duquette, camp manager, move her shelter away from a crevasse.

On May 11, one member of the German group contacted Reichert inquiring about a route on the North-West Face of Hunter. At that time Reichert told him that he believed the route had not been climbed and pointed out objective dangers due to seracs and cornices. (Post accident research revealed that the route had been climbed previously, see AAJ 1000, pp. 30-38.) Reichert and the German also talked about the dangerous snow conditions that existed below 12,000 feet throughout the range. The German concurred about snow conditions based on what they had found on the Kennedy-Lowe route, but believed that his proposed line would be mostly on ice and only subject to objective dangers for a minimum of time.

On May 12, Zitzewitz and Hecklinger made a foray to the base of the North-West Face of Hunter to break trail and get a closer look at their route. That evening Reichert spoke with one of the two about their plans and radio frequencies. Their FM radio was not compatible with other local frequencies, so they decided not to carry it. They planned to carry three days of food and fuel, minimal bivouac gear and ice climbing gear. They planned to leave at 0300 on May 13 and hoped to reach the end of the technical difficulties at 13,000 feet in one sustained push, sleep, and then descend the West Ridge.

At 0900 on May 13, Reichert located the duo through a spotting scope; they were moving well, climbing belayed pitches between 9,500 feet and 10,500 feet on the Northwest face. At 1100 people in base camp witnessed an avalanche on the Northwest Face of Hunter and reported it to Reichert, who located the climbers approximately 1,000 feet below the last seen spot. He could detect no movement. They were connected by their climbing rope. One was partially buried in a crevasse and the other was hanging.

At 1258 the LAMA helicopter lifted off from the 7,200 foot basecamp with helicopter manager David Kreutzer and Ranger Joe Reichert on board. Once all appropriate checks were made the green light was given to short-haul to the victims. At 1325 Reichert was lowered to the scene. He checked vital signs on both climbers and attached the bodies to the short-haul rope. Back at base camp, Ranger-medic Eric Martin confirmed that Zitzewitz and Hecklinger were deceased. Peter Fresia, a climbing partner, positively identified the bodies which were then transported to Talkeetna by Hudson Air Service.

Analysis
The Northwest Face of Mount Hunter is subject to objective dangers from cornice fall and avalanches. The approach to this face is extremely dangerous and has only been made twice before. It is impossible to say exactly what caused the avalanche that created this accident. There was a crown line approximately 400 feet above their high point that Reichert estimated to be two feet thick and 50 feet long. This could have been released sympathetically as the climbers moved from ice onto the snow slope or it could have been triggered by falling debris from above. There is a cornice overhanging the route at 13,000 feet.

The climbers were belaying each 165 foot pitch and appeared to have an ice ax anchor established at the belay and two ice screws placed for protection when the accident occurred. During the fall the victims passed over a rock band which probably caused the extensive trauma resulting in the fatalities. (Source: Denali National Park—Talkeetna Subdistrict Ranger Station)

FALL ON SNOW, INADEQUATE PROTECTION AND BELAY, HAPE, FROSTBITE
Alaska, Mount McKinley, South Buttress
On May 27, Nancy Bluhm (32) of the "Dancing Fools" expedition was airlifted by helicopter from the South Buttress of Mount McKinley after sustaining injuries from a 75 foot roped fall. The expedition flew on May 18 to the Kahiltna Glacier to climb the South Buttress. Expedition members included Tom Masterson (leader), Steve Parry, and Nancy Bluhm. The group reports climbing approximately 1000 feet a day up the Southeast Fork of the Kahiltna and on to the section of the South Buttress known as The Ramp. On May 27 the group left camp at 15,800 feet and descended into the col dividing the South Buttress from a steep head wall. The weather was unremarkable with minimal wind at 0 to 5 degrees F. While leading up the head wall Masterson climbed over a bergschrund and continued on with a running belay with Parry second on the rope. When Bluhm reached the bergschrund, a decision was made to stop and descend to the col. At 1430, Bluhm fell on the 40 degree snow slope generating enough force to pull Parry off his stance and slide 75 feet before being arrested by Masterson and a single ice ax anchor.

After the fall Tom lowered Parry to Bluhm. Parry reports that Bluhm was conscious, talking, but unable to move until her 40 pound pack was removed. Once the pack was removed Bluhm was able to walk over to the col while complaining of pain in one of her knees and her back. In the col the body of the tent was set up (the fly was lost in the fall) and Bluhm was placed in a sleeping bag and given fluids. Shortly after being stabilized she began displaying symptoms of shock. At 1630 Masterson and Parry attempted to contact the Talkeetna Ranger station and the Kahiltna base camp via cell phone. They tried repeatedly for over two hours, only getting the message, "Your cell phone is not authorized for this service–." Finally the group reached the State Troopers after calling 911. At 1927 the State Troopers made contact with the Talkeetna Ranger Station and were able to brief the Talkeetna staff and relay messages for the rest of the operation. The "Dancing Fools" expedition reported that they had one member with an injured back secondary to falling, one member with frostbite and symptoms of pulmonary edema, and that they had lost some equipment including a tent. At 2046 a fixed wing aircraft took off from the Talkeetna airstrip to act as cover ship for the NPS rescue helicopter. At 2056 the helicopter departed with pilot Doug Drury and Ranger Daryl Miller. By 2140, Drury had inspected the potential landing zone and reported winds at 30 knots out of the west with good visibility. As conditions appeared favorable the helicopter landed and took aboard Bluhm without the need for immediate medical attention. Masterson told Ranger Miller that Parry had a little frostbite and beginning signs of pulmonary edema but would try to descend the next day. A tent and C.B. radio were left with Masterson and Parry before flying Bluhm to the Kahiltna base camp. Bluhm was evaluated by NPS paramedic Eric Martin at the Kahiltna base camp and transported to Talkeetna by Jay Hudson where she was met by an ambulance which took her to Valley Hospital in Palmer, Alaska. Bluhm was released from the hospital the next day after being treated for a strained back and skin abrasions. No other injuries were reported.

Analysis
The length of this fall and the resulting injury may have been avoided by using more snow anchors during the running belay. An even better alternative would have been to use a sliding middle belay which would have enabled Bluhm to be lowered with a belay, Parry to descend a fixed line, and Masterson to descend with the same security of a running belay. Finally, the decision to continue on to the higher and more committing part of the route may not have been reasonable considering that one member was suffering from symptoms of pulmonary edema and minor frostbite. (Source: Billy Shott, Mountaineering Ranger)

FALL ON SNOW, INADEQUATE PROTECTION, CLIMBING UNROPED, INEXPERIENCE
Alaska, Mount McKinley, West Buttress.
On May 19, "Seven Summits Croatia" party of two flew into the Kahiltna Glacier with plans to summit Mt. McKinley via the Messner Couloir. They spent one day at 8000 feet, the third day at 11,000 feet, and the fourth at 14,000 feet. At this point they were forced to rest due to the rapid ascent and minor altitude sickness.

On the sixth day they reached 16,400 feet and rested a day to acclimatize better. Dolovski suffered minor headaches at this point. On the eighth day the two climbed to the 17,200-foot camp on the West Buttress to acclimate, then returned to 14,200 the following day and prepared to begin climbing early the next morning. A small high pressure system moved in and the weather was clear and cold. The two climbers left at 0200 on the tenth day to attempt the summit via the Messner Couloir. They reached the summit around 1330. At this point Ungar reports that the weather began to deteriorate. Both climbers agreed to descend via Denali Pass on the West Buttress route. Ungar reports that Dolovski was feeling strong so he took the lead. Both climbers agreed to descend unroped in order to facilitate a rapid descent and because they lacked the necessary equipment to protect the route.

At the Football Field the climbers found themselves in a whiteout and decided to follow a wanded route down the mountain. They followed the wands onto a steep slope between 40 and 60 degrees and decided that they must be off route, but could not determine where they were. At this time Ungar took the lead with Dolovski following only two meters behind. Ungar estimates that he reached a bench in the slope at 19,000 feet. and decided to reanalyze the descent. It was at this time that Ungar reports Dolovski's sudden fall past him and quickly out of sight. Ungar continued his descent, searching for his partner, hoping he had successfully self-arrested. Ungar eventually came to a fork on the Orient Express and decided to search the left couloir. When he found no sign, he climbed back up to the col and began descending the right gully towards the 16,200 foot camp.

Ungar was sighted descending the Orient Express at 2132. His elevation was estimated at 17,500 feet. The high altitude rescue helicopter was put on alert, awaiting a clearing in the weather at 2200 and launched at 2245 in order to assist with the rescue of the solo climber. A Colorado party made the initial contact with Ungar at 2255 and determined him to be okay but very tired. At 2333 Dr. Colin Grissom's team from the 14,200-foot camp reached Ungar with the initial two rescue teams at 15,000 feet, and determined that the rescue helicopter was unnecessary and that his team would escort Ungar back to 14,200.

Analysis
Both climbers had very little high altitude climbing experience prior to coming to the Alaska Range and had no prior experience on McKinley. Therefore, the route they chose was ambitious and maybe more technical than they expected. The small window of good weather they received the day prior to their summit day proved to be only temporary and they had no plan of how they would descend should the weather deteriorate, as it did, up high. They brought insufficient snow/ice anchors for their climb and descent and as a result did not use their rope at all. It is possible that had they been roped without anchors, both climbers would have died on the descent. But considering the long and difficult ascent, and high altitude, it would appear that the placement of anchors while descending would have been a safe way to go, especially upon discovering they were off route and on steep snow and ice. (Source: Billy Shott, Mountaineering Ranger)

FAULTY USE OF CRAMPON—FALL ON SNOW
Alaska, Mount McKinley
The Spanish expedition "Lleida McKinley '96" had eleven climbers in the group, including Juanjo Garra (32). They began their ascent of the West Buttress on May 19. On June 1 at 1300, while ascending above Denali Pass, Juanjo Garra lost a crampon causing him to fall. During the fall he sustained a comminuted fracture of the distal fibula. A Ranger patrol at 17,000 feet responded and lowered Garra to the 14,000 foot Ranger Camp where he was evacuated by a military Chinook helicopter on June 3.

Analysis
The terrain on the West Buttress of Denali above 11,000 feet is often steep, exposed, and underestimated. It is demanding on climbers' attention and equipment. Faulty use

of equipment has caused several falls on this terrain. Many first time climbers here are unfamiliar with the fit of their crampons to a pair of newly purchased overboots. Careful attention to the match and fit of this equipment is essential to safe climbing. This equipment should be tested in a controlled environment, and inspected frequently. (Source: Denali National Park - Talkeetna Subdistrict Ranger Station)

HACE
Alaska, Mount McKinley, West Buttress

On June 12, Ka Eui-Ryong of the Korean Alpine Club Su Won Expedition, was unable to stand or walk without assistance. Eui-Ryong was lowered from the 17,200 foot camp, to the 14,200 foot NPS Ranger Camp on the West Buttress. Eui-Ryong was diagnosed with high altitude cerebral edema by the NPS Patrol Doctor.

He was flown out on June 12 by the NPS LAMA helicopter to the 7,200 foot Kahiltna Base camp, transferred to an Air National Guard helicopter and flown to the Regional hospital in Anchorage.

Analysis

The Su Won Expedition spent seven days reaching the 14,200 foot camp and moved up two days later. Eui-Ryong was suffering from AMS at 14,200 feet before he moved up to the 17,200 foot camp and never fully acclimated the rest of the time he spent on the mountain. Returning to the high camp at 17,200 feet was a guarantee that he would be susceptible to HAPE or HACE. The Su Won expedition, like many others, put the summit ahead of personal safety. They underestimated both the altitude and the scale of Mt. McKinley. (Source: Denali National Park - Talkeetna Subdistrict Ranger Station)

FALLING ROCK, STRANDED
Alaska, Alaska Range, Coffee Glacier, Eyetooth

On June 15, JJ Brooks (33) was hit by fragments from a large falling rock that had separated from the main rock face. The falling rock had also cut his climbing rope, stranding him and his partner, Carl Tobin, four pitches up. They established verbal contact. Brooks, though seriously injured, was able to use a fragment of the rope to set up a series of short rappels that eventually got him to within 15-20 feet of the glacier. He let himself go at that point, hit the snow and slid, launching himself over the bergschrund to the snow below. He was able to make his way back to their camp, where he took some pain killers and attempted to stabilize his injuries. Tobin yelled from the wall above, "Ski out," and then threw his pack down to provide Brooks with more warm clothing. Brooks began a slow, painful descent, knowing that a couple of other teams, Jim Sweeney and his partner, and Alex Lowe and Steve Swenson, were camped two miles away near the air strip. Both Tobin and Brooks yelled off and on to attract attention. Sweeney heard the yells. Lowe and Swenson got to Brooks, made radio contact and began stabilizing him and preparing a sled to transport him to camp. Sweeney stayed with Brooks in camp.

At 2:00 am the next morning. Swenson and Lowe skied up the glacier to the base of the route. At sunrise they began their ascent to help Carl Tobin, who had spent a chilly night on his ledge.

On June 17, after radio contact with an overhead locator had finally made contact, a Pavehawk helicopter from the 210 Air National Guard picked up Lowe and Brooks at

1843 and flew them to Anchorage Regional Hospital. JJ Brooks was found to have a fractured—in fact, shattered—humeral head, possible rib fracture, ankle sprain, and possible concussion. (The reason for Alex Lowe flying out was that when he and Swenson climbed up to get Tobin, he felt some urinary tract discomfort, and by the time they all returned to Brooks, he noticed blood in his urine. He was diagnosed as having a kidney infection, which may or may not have been a result of a long fall he took while negotiating an aid route on an overhang from the Eyetooth, where he and Swenson were attempting a new line.)

Brooks required an operation that has left him with a prosthetic shoulder, and his middle deltoid was shredded.

Analysis
The 1996 climbing season was particularly warm. The unusual heat melted much of the ice that normally stabilized rocks along many Alaska Range climbs. It is to be noted that Brooks' self extrication under the circumstances was extraordinary. But it is also fortunate that Swenson and Lowe, who had originally intended to climb in a different part of the range, happened to be on hand in this remote, not-often-visited area. (Source: From a report sent by Steve Swenson, and Jed Williamson)

APPENDICITIS
Alaska, Mount McKinley, Muldrow Glacier
On June 19 at 2345, a National Outdoor Leadership School expedition requested a helicopter to evacuate a sick student located at 7,200 feet on the Muldrow Glacier.

At 0900 that day, Tilney felt nauseous, and had abdominal pain located in the lower right quadrant. At the time they were carrying loads. Tilney's symptoms got worse, so the expedition stopped at 1400 and made camp at 7,200 feet. Tilney's symptoms included vomiting, fever of 102 F, and continued severe pain localized in the lower right quadrant of the abdomen. NOLS leaders, who have EMT and Wilderness First Responder Training, determined that Tilney was most likely suffering from appendicitis. Tilney was given two Pepto-Bismol and then rested. The leaders used a cell phone to contact the NOLS headquarters in Palmer. They contacted Denali National Park requesting an evacuation of Tilney. The NOLS expedition prepared a helicopter landing zone near their camp site. This landing zone later proved to be advantageous to the pilot.

At 2345 the Talkeetna Ranger Station was contacted and the LAMA helicopter along with a cover ship was dispatched. A uniform cloud layer with a ceiling at 9,500 feet obstructed most of the range. A favorable route was found that allowed the aircraft's access to the Muldrow glacier. The NOLS expedition carried an aircraft radio enabling air to ground communication, and the aircraft zeroed in on their location. The landing zone was encircled by weighted duffels and packs allowing the LAMA pilot to identify it in poor visibility.

Tilney was picked up at 0205 and transported to Talkeetna at 0239. He was given an IV, transferred to Life Flight, and flown to Alaska Regional Hospital. He was admitted to surgery for an appendectomy.

Analysis
Tilney's evacuation was precisely executed due to several factors. First, the ability to recognize the signs and symptoms of appendicitis. Second, the communication equip-

ment carried by the NOLS expedition allowed them to contact help from a remote area. Expeditions prepared for the worst case scenario increase their probability of avoiding a disaster in the field. (Source: Denali National Park—Talkeetna Subdistrict Ranger Station)

UNKNOWN, CLIMBING UNROPED, PLACED NO PROTECTION, FAILURE TO TURN BACK, WEATHER
Alaska, Mount McKinley, West Buttress

On June 2, Karl Jendryschik and Jurgen Bruhm of the German expedition Saxonia 96, were separated from each other at Denali Pass. At 2252 Jendryschik contacted an NPS patrol at 17,000 feet and told them his partner Bruhm did not make it down from Denali Pass. Jendryschik thought Bruhm either fell or bivouacked at the pass. A ground and air search was suspended periodically because of weather. On June 14, the search for Bruhm was reactivated as the weather improved. Bruhm was not located and is presumed deceased. Rescuers hoped that Bruhm had survived a three day bivouac during the June 3 to 7 period. There was no evidence to support this theory except for a used chemical heat pack that could have been used by Bruhm during his bivouac with Jendryschik on June 2. According to an interview with Jendryschik, Bruhm was not accomplished in the skill of self arrest. Their exposure to big mountains and severe cold weather was shallow, and they felt extended.

Analysis

The Saxonian expedition overextended themselves in attempting the summit. The weather obviously was not optimal during their summit attempt and the forecast predicted higher winds, from what already could be considered as dreadful conditions. They should have turned back instead of attempting the summit.

The weather forecast is a weighty factor in making the decision on whether to go up or not. The forecast should also be interpreted as conservatively as one's nature permits. Whether having a radio would have helped them in receiving the weather forecast is unknown, as Jendryschik's English was poor.

Many falls have occurred at Denali Pass and will no doubt continue, until climbers use protection on this terrain. Pickets are very easy to carry and place on the traverse. Their use adds a tremendous safeguard for climbers descending the pass.

FALL ON SNOW, CLIMBING ALONE and HAPE, HACE
Alaska, Mount McKinley, West Buttress

Chihiro Sakamaki flew to the Kahiltna base camp on June 10 and immediately began climbing the West Buttress reaching the 14,200 foot camp within 10 days. By June 19, Sakamaki had established his camp at 17,200 feet. He began his summit attempt on the next day. Sakamaki reached approximately 19,000 feet and began descending for unknown reasons. During his descent Sakamaki fell around the 18,500 foot level in an area known as The Autobahn. He went a distance of 1000 feet, losing a total of 300 vertical feet. He was experiencing pain throughout his thoracic region, but was able to continue his descent.

On arrival at his 17,200 foot camp he contacted guide Vern Tejas and told him of his injuries. At 2120 Tejas contacted the base camp manager Annie Duquette and reported Sakamaki's situation. At 2133, Duquette contacted the Talkeetna Ranger station and reported to Ranger Kevin Moore. Ranger Daryl Miller, located at the 14,200-foot camp was then given the message, and he contacted the 17,200 foot camp. It was decided that Sakamaki was seriously injured and would need evacuation. Weather conditions at this time were mostly clear at 14,000 feet and above, but cloudy with whiteout conditions below which prevented any flights until the next day.

Meanwhile, the "AAI 2" expedition, led by Mimi Bourquin, arrived at the Kahiltna base camp on June 4. The expedition reached the 14,200 foot camp on June 14 and had established a camp at 17,200 feet by June 18. The group was feeling and moving well. On June 19 the expedition made a summit bid. At 1500, after reaching the 19,000 foot level, client Debbie Sherman complained of a severe headache and began displaying odd behavior. Bourquin immediately descended with Sherman, who was ambulatory, and arrived at the 17,200 foot camp around 1750. Bourquin and Sherman continued descending and arrived at the 14,200 foot Ranger camp at 2100. Sherman was evaluated by medical personnel and held in the medical tent for continued treatment and observation. Sherman's condition continued to worsen with increasing periods of unconsciousness, ataxia, and confusion. Plans were made to evacuate as soon as weather would permit.

On June 21 at 0935, the Park Service LAMA helicopter departed Talkeetna. At 1021 the LAMA helicopter picked up Ranger Miller at the 14,200 foot camp and departed to pick up Sakamaki. At 1039 the LAMA helicopter returned to the 14,200-foot camp with Ranger Miller and Sakamaki, picked up Sherman, and continued to the 7,000-foot base camp. At 1123, pilot Jay Hudson took aboard Sherman, Sakamaki, and Paramedic Ranger Eric Martin, and flew to Talkeetna where both patients were transferred to Alaska Regional Hospital via Flight for Life helicopter. Sakamaki was treated for broken ribs and released after three days. Sherman was held overnight for observation as her symptoms of high altitude pulmonary and cerebral edema subsided.

Analysis

The "AAI 2" expedition never gained more than 1000 feet per day, which is generally the safe rate of ascent in avoiding altitude illnesses. However, it is not uncommon for individuals to begin suffering from HAPE or HACE during or after a summit attempt regardless of how acclimatized they are. In addition, though small groups are statistically at more risk of obtaining an altitude illness from ascending too rapidly, large groups are also at an increased risk as members may be less likely to report early symptoms of altitude sickness.

The area in which Sakamaki fell has been the sight of numerous falls with injuries ranging from twisted ankles to head injuries. This section is not technically difficult but is steeper than surrounding terrain and often very icy. Sakamaki may have been able to avoid his accident simply by using more caution and slowing down, since climbing solo did not allow any type of practical belay. If Sakamaki had not been able to walk after his fall the consequences would have been far worse as there were few, if any, climbers descending behind him. (Source: Billy Shott, Mountaineering Ranger)

CRAMPON PROBLEM, INEXPERIENCE
Alaska, Mount McKinley, West Buttress

On June 8, the "Love Mountain and Beer" party of three Japanese climbers flew in to climb the West Buttress. They reached the summit on June 21 at 1620 in very good weather conditions. They were several hundred meters from reaching their high camp

(17,400 feet) when at 1830, Takeshi Nagao caught a crampon on his overboot causing him to twist and fall on his back. Nagao injured his left leg and ankle in the fall. He was last on the rope, sliding five meters on the 30 degree slope. Nagao felt a lot of pain when he put weight on his ankle. The two other team members assisted Nagao to camp, arriving at 1900. Once in camp they consulted Fantasy Ridge guide Vern Tejas. Tejas examined Nagao. He instructed his party to begin applying ice on the injury. At 2030, Tejas reported the incident by radio to Ranger Daryl Miller at the 14,200 foot Ranger Station. Tejas suspected Nagao had a broken leg due to its appearance and location of pain. He reported that Nagao would need assistance in getting down. They would check back in the morning.

Nagao felt he had only sprained his ankle and by resting several days he would be able to descend on his own power. On June 22 at 0800, Tejas examined Nagao and he found him to be in a lot of pain and non-ambulatory. Tejas convinced Nagao that he had a serious injury and that it would not get better by waiting. Nagao agreed with Tejas that he should be evacuated from the 17,200 foot camp.

At 0850, Tejas radioed the 14,200 foot camp, reporting that Nagao's condition was unchanged and felt that he either needed to be lowered or helicopter evacuated. With the good weather conditions, Ranger Miller felt a helicopter evacuation would be the safest means to evacuate Nagao. Nagao was picked up at 1309 and was transported to Talkeetna, and was then transported by ambulance to Valley Hospital in Palmer. Nagao had broken his left fibula.

Analysis

This is another example of a climber using equipment that is unfamiliar. The combination of crampons on overboots, altitude, and, most likely, fatigue increase the probability of this kind of mishap, though it is unusual that the resulting injury is as serious as this one was. (Source: Jed Williamson)

(Editor's Note: It seems that evacuation from this altitude is becoming more common.)

AVALANCHE, POOR POSITION—UNDER OBJECTIVE HAZARDS
Alaska, Mount Hunter, West Face

At 2400 on June 21, Chuck Drake (27) and Joshua Hane (28) departed the 7,200-foot Kahiltna Base Camp. They were attempting to climb a previously unclimbed route on the West Face of Mt. Hunter, with a return down the West Ridge. They were using an alpine style ascent, carrying only four days food and fuel, bivvy sacks and down parkas. Weather conditions were favorable for the first two days, but deteriorated significantly on the third day. The climbers were reported overdue by park rangers on June 27. Aerial search and ground observation efforts were initiated at 1018 on June 27. Weather conditions severely limited flying and search activities until the 30th. A total of 42.8 hours of fixed wing and helicopter overflights were conducted for the next week. Rangers flying in the LAMA helicopter reported sighting a body. Further observation of the area by ground and aerial spotters revealed the area too hazardous to attempt a recovery operation.

On July 7, Drake's body was swept approximately 1,000 feet to the bottom of the avalanche cone. Spotters watching the accident site concurred that a body recovery was possible if conducted in the early morning.

Analysis

Hane and Drake had previously climbed in the Alaska Range, and both were experienced mountaineers. They had prior knowledge of the poor snow and ice conditions before attempting their climb, including information regarding the two German climbers who had died in an avalanche several weeks earlier.

They climbed up to the 16,200 foot camp on the West Buttress, and were cautioned about the poor conditions on Mt. Hunter by the rangers. Their intended route was extremely dangerous objectively, with abundant rockfall, along with ice and snow avalanches cascading down on a routine basis.

The mechanism seems to have been that both climbers were hit by avalanche debris from above while rappelling the route. There are many unanswered questions, especially the selection of the route itself. Approaching the climb from the bottom, it would have been difficult for them not to notice the hundreds of craters from the rocks, and the huge ice hangers above them.

In 1996, Mt. Hunter had 20 expeditions attempt to reach the summit, with the results being no summits and four fatalities. (Source: Billy Schott, Mountaineering Ranger)

FALL INTO CREVASSE, INADEQUATE EXTRICATION PROCEDURE
Alaska, Mount McKinley, Ruth Glacier

On June 16, all six members of the French "Wayne's World" expedition including Thomas Roques, Jean Jacques Peladeix, Jacqueline Peladeix, Michelle Pertuis, Jean Pierre Pertuis, and expedition leader Peter Dutrievoz were airlifted by helicopter from the Ruth Glacier after Michelle Pertuis (50) sustained injuries from a fall into and then extrication from a crevasse.

The expedition had planned ten days to travel from the Don Sheldon Amphitheater, down the Ruth Glacier, and to exit it by following Alder Creek to the Tokositna River where they were to meet guide Michael Overcast with a raft and float out to Talkeetna. On July 14, after being flown to the Mountain House air strip by Hudson Aviation, the group traveled by foot pulling sleds approximately one mile down glacier and made camp. On the 15th, the group continued down glacier and at 1300, Michelle Pertuis fell in a crevasse. Leader Dutrievoz reports that Michelle fell up to her waist and was extracted by the other rope team members simply by pulling her out without using any pulley system. Once out of the crevasse Michelle reported sharp pains in her upper left quadrant. The group made camp shortly after this incident near the base of Mt. Dickey. While at this camp Dutrievoz reports that Michelle tripped and fell which may have exacerbated her abdominal injury. On July 16, the expedition attempted to continue down glacier. Michelle was unable to carry any weight and continued to complain of sharp pain.

At 1250 air taxi Doug Geeting Aviation dispatch relayed that the pilot Doug Geeting, while on a scenic flight, had received a request for helicopter evacuation from a group on the Ruth Glacier. The Talkeetna Ranger Station contacted the Rescue Coordination Center at 1330 and at 1400 a Pavehawk helicopter was en route to the accident site. At 1509 a 185 Cessna contracted from K2 Aviation was launched as cover ship from Talkeetna with Pilot Richard Almsted, Ranger Joe Reichert, and Ken Zaffren, M.D., aboard. At 1530 the Air Force helicopter landed and picked up all six members of the expedition and flew them directly to Alaska Regional Hospital in Anchorage, where Michelle Pertuis was treated and released with thoracic and kidney bruising.

Analysis

Expedition leader Peter Dutrievoz reported that Pertuis' fall into the crevasse was slow and nondynamic and that she did not experience any pain until she was pulled out of the crevasse. Injuries might have been avoided if more time and less force were used in extracting Pertuis from the crevasse.

Evacuation of all six members was not necessary. Dutrievoz stated he did not want to send Pertuis out alone due to her anxiety and language barrier and that group morale was too low to continue. Neither of these reasons would warrant evacuation of more than the injured person in most rescue situations in the Alaska Range. However, this appears to be a difference in perception by Europeans, who are used to frequent helicopter evacs (NB: 800 missions a year average out of Zermatt alone), and who have rescue insurance. (Source: Billy Shott, Mountaineering Ranger)

(Editor's Note: This provides us with another example of why we should charge such parties for the costs of rescue.)

16' FALL INTO CREVASSE—WITH WATER AT THE BOTTOM, UNABLE TO EXTRICATE—INADEQUATE PEOPLE POWER, HYPOTHERMIA
Alaska, Mount McKinley, West Buttress

On June 21, a guided party, led by guides Chris Morris and Stacy Taniguchi flew onto the Kahiltna Glacier to begin a climb of the West Buttress route. Among the seven clients was Dennis Gum. During the following 14 days the group progressed up to the 14,200 foot level. While camped at 11,200 feet and 14,200 feet Dennis Gum was having difficulties sleeping due to chain stokes breathing. Making a carry to the 16,200 foot camp on July 4, Gum became exhausted and decided to retreat. He was accompanied by Taniguchi to the 14,200 foot camp. On July 5, Taniguchi and Morris decided to have Gum leave the mountain. Due to the location of the team at 14,200 feet, it was not feasible to have a team descend with Gum and then attempt to return. So it was decided that Taniguchi would descend along with Gum, and depart the mountain as well.

Taniguchi and Gum departed the 14,200-foot camp at 1145 on July 5. By 1800 they were at the 8,000 foot level where Taniguchi decided to stop in order to rest, eat, drink and wait for the coolness of evening to firm up the snow. At 2330 it began to snow and Taniguchi decided to continue their descent to avoid losing the trail even though the surface snow had only a slight crust. The duo recommenced traveling at 0030 on July 6. They were both on snowshoes, with Taniguchi traveling in front. Whiteout conditions persisted as they followed the trail. Taniguchi remembers taking a break at 0430.

At some point during the following hour Taniguchi punched both legs through a snow bridge and was able to crawl out. He instructed Gum to maintain a tight rope and not to follow his tracks at that point. When he arrived at the hidden crevasse, Gum opted to attempt crossing several feet to the west of the trail and when he stepped onto the snow bridge it failed, sending Gum into the crevasse. Due to the weight difference (Gum is approximately 80 pounds heavier, and gear added another 40), Taniguchi was unable to arrest the fall. Gum fell approximately 45 feet and landed in water. Taniguchi was able to use a picket and ice ax to make an anchor, escape the belay and go to the edge to investigate. At first he could only make voice contact due to the darkness in the hole, so Taniguchi lowered a parka and mittens and instructed Gum to begin ascending the rope. The mittens did not fit and Gum could not make his ascending system work, so Taniguchi began heating water and setting up a haul system. Taniguchi was unable to raise Gum, so he instructed him to sit on his pack and sled to be out of the water. For the next four hours Taniguchi concentrated his efforts on heating water for Gum, which he would lower into the crevasse in a thermos, talking with him to maintain Gum's consciousness and calling for help on the CB radio. Several planes flew over, but Taniguchi's call was not hailed.

It was approximately 0950 when Joe Reichert heard the Mayday call on the radio. Reichert reported the call to the Talkeetna ranger station and requested that the LAMA rescue helicopter launch, earlier than its 1100 hour scheduled mission, to provide back-up for the ground rescue. Taniguchi and Reichert talked several times on the CB about patient condition and gear requirements. Reichert and Nancy Juergens packed rescue gear, fuel and a synthetic, medical sleeping bag and departed base camp on skis at 1025. Reichert and Juergens arrived on scene at 1050. Juergens unpacked and sorted gear while Taniguchi belayed Reichert to the lip of the crevasse where Reichert surveyed the accident and established communication with Gum. Deadman-style anchors were constructed using skis and pickets. The hole on the downhill edge of the crevasse was enlarged and the edge was padded with skis. Reichert then lowered Gum a new rope and instructed him to clip in. Taniguchi, Reichert and Juergens were then able to raise Gum out of the water utilizing a Z-system for mechanical advantage.

At 1130, the LAMA was on scene rigged for a short-haul operation. Reichert lowered the short-haul line to Gum who connected it to his waist harness. As the LAMA raised Gum further, Reichert observed that Gum was horizontal and his backpack and sled were hanging off him. Reichert instructed the LAMA to hover, instructed Taniguchi and Juergens to take up the slack on the primary haul system, and Reichert rigged a rappel line and descended to Gum. On his way down Reichert cut the original rope because it was through the original hole and in the way of the operation. Upon reaching Gum, Reichert secured himself to the rappel rope and hooked into the short-haul line. Reichert then cut the pack and sled free from Gum and lifted his torso into an upright position. Reichert instructed the LAMA to start raising as he held Gum's legs from below to maintain the upright position. With Taniguchi at the hole giving hand signals and Reichert on the radio, Drury was able to slowly bring the two safely to the surface. Gum and Reichert were set down on the snow and the LAMA landed, Gum was loaded aboard the ship and flown to base camp where Kreutzer and Drury transported him to the weather-port using a cascade litter, removed his clothes and packaged him in multiple sleeping bags with numerous hot water bottles. Drury then returned to pick up Reichert, Taniguchi and Juergens.

Between 1200 and 1430, Gum was treated for hypothermia. His vital signs were recorded at regular intervals and a secondary examination was performed by Reichert to investigate possible additional injuries. Gum complained of lower back soreness and had a large bruise on his left leg quadriceps muscle. At 1446 Gum was transported via Pavehawk helicopter to Alaska Regional Hospital.

Analysis

Gum developed hypothermia because he was in the crevasse and wet for over five hours. The contributing factors to this serious situation were falling into a crevasse and the not being able to perform an extrication. On this particular day when the surface snow had not frozen the group knew that crevasse hazards were high. Therefore extra care could have been taken by Gum to probe with his ski pole, especially in light of Taniguchi falling in just before him. Once the accident occurred it was Taniguchi's responsibility, as the leader, to make an extrication happen. The substantial difference in weight made this very difficult. Extra people power would have resolved this problem, hence the decision by a guide to travel on the glacier with only one client, although many teams of two climb McKinley each season, must be evaluated more thoroughly in the future. Perhaps Gum could have waited at a higher camp for the group to make their summit attempt and then descend as a team.

Despite having practiced ascending a rope at the beginning of the expedition, Gum encountered complications that he could not overcome to ascend out of the crevasse himself. Taniguchi attempted to rig a Z-pulley system but due to limited gear he could not build enough mechanical advantage to raise Gum. While in the crevasse Gum could have helped his situation by putting on a fleece hat that was in a side pouch of his pack and eating snacks from the top of his pack. One medical complication which was discovered at the hospital was that Gum's potassium level was ten points below normal. This occurred because he ingested such a large quantity of hot water. The warmth provided by this water undoubtedly contributed to his survival, but the addition of a flavor mix to the water would have helped even more. (Source: Denali National Park—Talkeetna Subdistrict Ranger Station)

RAPPEL ERROR—ROPE NOT ANCHORED, NO BELAY
Arizona, Oak Creek Canyon
On April 13, Benjamin Rusev (19) fell 75 feet down a cliff in Oak Creek Canyon. At the time, he was attempting to rappel. Rusev's partner tried to grab the line after Rusev began falling.

Many other people were climbing in the area—one of the most popular climbing spots near Flagstaff—when Rusev fell. (The overlook is about eight miles south of Flagstaff.) One of them was a registered nurse, Jeff Davis, who works at Flagstaff Medical Center. Davis and other climbers cared for Rusev while rescue teams headed to the scene. Eleven members of the Coconino County Sheriff's Search and Rescue Team responded, as did Kachina Village firefighters and an Arizona Department of Public Safety air-rescue team. (Source: *Arizona Daily Sun*, April 4, 1996)

(Editor's Note: Angelo Kokenakis, a mountain guide from Flagstaff, reported in a letter that the usual beginning climbing area of this crag had been closed off for safety reasons—to protect the non-climbing public who use the crag as a vista lookout. So these neophytes were actually using an unknown 80 foot crag rather than the established 30 foot beginner area.)

CLIMBING ALONE and UNROPED, DISTRAUGHT
Arkansas, Sam's Throne
On October 12, Chris Harris (23) was soloing at night on Instant Trauma (5.10a) when he fell 75 feet to his death.

Analysis
Harris came out late in the afternoon, and was supposed to meet friends. But they didn't show up. He took all his gear—rope, solo aid device, etc.—and laid it out neatly at the bottom of the cliff. However, when he was found, it was obvious that he didn't

use any of it. It was also known that he had several unresolved personal problems which may have had an effect on his actions. (Source: Mark Allen)

FALL ON ROCK, CLIMBING ALONE AND UNROPED
California, Morro Bay, Morro Rock

On January 21, Jody Walker (17) of St. Helena died from head and neck injuries after he plunged about 100 feet from Morro Rock while climbing its northwest face.

"When our paramedics got to him he was unconscious," said Morro Bay Fire Chief Jeff Jones. "He suffered significant blood loss."

Jones had worked with the Morro Bay Fire Department since 1979 and said he can't remember anyone dying in a rock-climbing incident at Morro Rock.

"If it's not the first, it's the first in a long time," he said.

Walker and his friend Justin Valasquez, also of St. Helena, were free climbing the Rock Sunday morning when Walker fell.

The 578-foot high rock is treacherous, said Dave Sears, spokesman for California State Parks, which manages Morro Rock. He said signs prohibiting climbers are posted near the Rock. Morro Rock is a peregrine falcon preserve and it is against the law to scale it, he said.

"The signs are there for their own protection," he said.

Several agencies participated in the rescue. Jones said even with the best training and professional equipment, rescuers can't save every accident victim. He urged the public to respect signs posted around the Rock. (Source: *San Luis Obispo County Telegram Tribune*, January 23, 1996)

(Editor's Note: This is the first report from Morro Rock. In nearby San Luis Obispo, there is a popular climbing cliff—complete with poison oak, snakes, owls, etc. Any additional information from this area will be appreciated.)

FALL ON ROCK, ROPE SEVERED, CARABINER BROKE
California, Yosemite Valley, El Capitan

On April 1, Matt Baxter (26), an experienced big-wall climber, set out alone to fix the first few pitches of Zenyatta Mondatta, a difficult multi-day aid route on El Capitan. The next morning, after he had failed to return home, friends found his body at the base of the route. He had apparently fixed the first two pitches and fallen while leading the third.

The first half of the third pitch slants up left at about 65 degrees on a vertical wall. The climbing is mostly on hooks and fixed copperheads, with an occasional camming device. Few placements offer bombproof protection. The equipment on Baxter's body—harness, daisies, etriers, hardware racks, and rope—was properly rigged, but the rope, a new Mammut Flash 10.5mm, was severed about 25 feet from the clove hitch he was using for an adjustable self-belay.

The other end of the rope, 15-20 feet long, was anchored at the start of the pitch and then clipped through a TCU 10-12 feet above and left of the belay. From there the rope ran 5 feet left across the top of a 2-foot wide pedestal and was jammed into a 1/4-in. wide crack between the pedestal and the wall. It had broken where it exited the crack on the far side of the pedestal, and was stretched tight between the belay, the TCU, and the crack.

The next placement, five to six feet above and left of the TCU and 3-4 feet directly above the pedestal, was a fixed copperhead from which hung one of Baxter's Quickdraws. The carabiner in the rope end of the Quickdraw, a Chouinard Bentgate Quicksilver, was broken, with the nose end missing. The route continued up and left from the copperhead, but the Quickdraw appeared to be the last of Baxter's hardware still in place.

Analysis

Based on the gear we found on the ground, and on the length of rope between the harness and the break, Baxter was probably 10-20 feet past the Quickdraw when he fell. An old fixed copperhead and possibly one or more hook placements failed, then a small camming device just above the Quickdraw pulled, followed by the failure of the carabiner. Since Baxter had fallen from a point to the left of the pedestal, and the TCU was to the right, the rope fell across the pedestal and into the crack.

Why did the rope break? A few inches of glazed, abraded, and ripped sheath on Baxter's side of the break suggest that the rope had been partially cut by being compressed against the rough sides of the crack and pulled through it by the force of the fall. The high friction increased the fall factor, so the rope between Baxter and the crack now had to absorb most or all of the remaining energy; it was more than the damaged core could handle, and it broke.

Would an intact carabiner have kept the rope out of the crack, or at least prevented the break? Probably so, though we did not test this. The rope would still have swung against the pedestal, but from a safer angle. In fact, it must have been in this position while the carabiner was still whole and the force was increasing (a fraction of a second), yet that section of rope showed no damage.

Why did the carabiner break? Steve Nagode and Chris Harmston, the Quality Assurance Managers of REI and Black Diamond Equipment, respectively, examined the broken carabiner. They reported that the material in the carabiner was of good quality, there were no preexisting cracks or other flaws in the piece remaining, and the distortions present were typical of a break occurring while the gate was open.

They also felt that two or three fresh, deep gouges on the back and side of the spine of the carabiner indicated that the spine had struck the wall during the impact. This would have opened the gate, dropping the strength of the carabiner to roughly a third of its rated value, at the moment the peak force occurred. (Slap the spine of a carabiner against your palm, and listen for the "click" of the gate opening and snapping shut.)

The "spine impact" mechanism requires that the carabiner be clipped to the rope in the standard gate-out configuration. However, because of the orientation of the copperhead and the Quickdraw to the rock surface, we could not determine how the broken carabiner had been clipped at the time of the accident.

Baxter had clipped the previous carabiner (on the TCU) down-and-in, so, at the scene, I replaced the broken carabiner with an identical one and clipped my own rope through it down-and-in. When I yanked on my rope to simulate the direction of force from Baxter's fall, the carabiner slid along the rope, seeking the equilibrium point, as expected. Since the rope held the gate against the rock, friction between the moving carabiner and the rock opened the gate and kept it open. I was surprised by how easily this occurred; however, if this had happened to Baxter's carabiner we should have found scratches on the gate, and there were none. The gouges on the spine make "spine impact" the more likely culprit in this case. (A simple "sticky gate" scenario is not likely since the gate moved freely after the accident.)

Although we don't know the actual force on the carabiner, Baxter and his gear weighed 225 pounds and his belay absorbed little energy—his clove hitch did not slip and there was no belayer or force-limiting belay device at the anchor to reduce the impact. The carabiner probably met its design specifications but, like the rope, was overwhelmed.

Carabiner failures are pretty rare. Harmston knows of only half-a-dozen out of several hundred thousand Chouinard and Black Diamond units sold, and they were all due to open gates. Nevertheless, current models, whether the traditional design or the newer wire gate type, seek to reduce the effects of "spine impact" by stiffening the gate spring and/or decreasing the mass of the gate.

While the chance of a carabiner failure or the rope unclipping is low, don't hesitate to use two reversed and opposed carabiners if you suspect a critical situation like this one. Perhaps more important, back up the placement itself if you can—a fixed copperhead or piton is more likely to fail than the carabiner.

We are all eager to hear about equipment "failures", but it's important to get the facts right: preserve what's left of the gear (don't touch freshly broken surfaces, for example), get the names of participants, photograph or draw the scene if possible, and notify the manufacturer. (Source: John Dill, NPS Ranger, Yosemite National Park; Steve Nagode, REI; Chris Harmston, Black Diamond Equipment, Ltd.)

STRANDED, INADEQUATE CLOTHING AND EQUIPMENT, WEATHER
California, Yosemite Valley, El Capitan
On May 16, 1996, the National Park Service rescued Austrian climbers Christian Zenz (22) and Christian Wassertheurer (27) from The Shield on El Capitan, after the pair had been exposed to a storm without a fly for their portaledge.

The pair got advice about the route from friends and from Yosemite Climbs. Zenz had also read the guide book chapter entitled "Staying Alive," which describes Yosemite storms and tactics for surviving them.

On Sunday morning, May 12, they checked the weather forecast, which called for sunny skies with a slight cooling trend, and started climbing. By Tuesday night they had completed one pitch above the Shield Roof. Tuesday was windy and cloudy but, in their opinion, not indicative of a storm. This was the first hanging bivouac they had encountered on the climb, and the first time they had needed their borrowed portaledge. When they set it up, they discovered that there was no rain fly. It rained that night, but they stayed fairly dry by using plastic tube tents over their sleeping bags.

The rain stopped Wednesday morning, allowing them to dry their clothes and sleeping bags in the breeze. They had 11 pitches to go, it was still cloudy, and without the fly they were completely exposed to further bad weather. Retreat was an option. The 25-foot roof would be difficult to down climb, but it was fixed and they had a cheater stick. However they thought the weather might improve, so they decided to continue up.

About 1400, before they could begin climbing, the rain began again. This time it was heavy, with a strong wind that blew their portaledge around. The wind and rain, mixed with sleet, continued through the night, and the temperature dipped below freezing with ice coating the wall. They were now soaking wet and very cold, in the "hardest" bivvy of their careers.

Wassertheurer was using a down sleeping bag. It was rated to well below freezing but it became useless as it got wet. They wore Gore-tex storm jackets and pants but claimed that the wind blew water through the fabric. Although they now realized they should rappel, their hands had become too cold to operate carabiners and they would certainly deteriorate further if they tried to descend. Thursday morning, knowing they were trapped, they called for a rescue.

The rain stopped by midday. After attempts to deliver a portaledge and bivvy gear by helicopter were thwarted by strong downdrafts, the rescue team was flown to the summit and one rescuer lowered to them. Zenz and Wassertheurer were able to jumar about 1000 feet to the rim without difficulty.

Analysis

Zenz and Wassertheurer each had eight years of climbing experience and climbed 5.13. They had climbed in many parts of the world, on multi-day routes, in rain, snow, wind, and cold temperatures. They had climbed the Nose on El Capitan just prior to attempting the Shield.

They stated later that they had borrowed the portaledge in Austria and had assumed the fly was in the same sack as the ledge; when they packed for the climb they did not attempt to check its condition, let alone that it was there in the first place. They agreed that they would have borrowed a rain fly before starting the climb, had they known theirs was missing.

Down is well known to lose almost all insulative value when wet. Wassertheurer relied on the shell material because it was supposed to be "highly water-resistant." He had apparently never tested it in truly wet conditions. Neither climber had bivvy sacks. We recommend (but do not guarantee) them as a second line of defense against condensation or leaks inside a portaledge.

Zenz and Wassertheurer were cited by the NPS for "creating a hazardous condition" by unnecessarily putting rescuers at risk, under 36 CFR 2.34 (a) (4). They pled guilty and were placed on one year's probation on the condition that they pay rescue costs totaling $13,325. (Source: Keith Lober, John Dill, NPS Rangers, Yosemite National Park)

ACUTE MOUNTAIN SICKNESS (AMS), PARTY SEPARATED, WEATHER
California, Mount Shasta

On May 25, Mike Turegun (35) and John Cain (49) approached Mount Shasta via Northgate, setting up a base camp at 9,000 feet on the bench near the Hotlum/Bolam Route. On May 26 they began climbing the Hotlum/Bolam Route. They left a pack with clothing, food, and insulin for Cain on the "step" at 12,000 feet and continued up the route. At 1400, Cain became altitude sick at 13,000 feet and stopped climbing. Cain wanted to turn back, so Turegun continued on to the summit (14,163 feet). As Turegun was returning to where he left Cain, a sudden snow storm hit, causing a whiteout. Turegun was unable to find the descent route and was guided back to his base camp by yelling to another climbing party. When Cain did not return to base camp by the next morning, Turegun walked out to their vehicle and drove to the USFS Ranger Station in Mount Shasta to report Cain missing. Cain was described as being in good physical condition with a lot of outdoor experience, having climbed Mount Shasta in the past via the Avalanche Gulch route. However, he was diabetic and also had mid-range multiple sclerosis. He wore braces on both legs below the knees.

Siskiyou County Sheriff Search and Rescue (SAR) team was contacted and a search was initiated, coordinated by Sgt. Dave Nickelson. At 1530 the pack left by Turegun and Cain was spotted on the step where they had left it by CHP helicopter and the base camp was overflown and was still unoccupied. Checks of other trailheads and roads yielded no results. At 2040 the search was halted and arrangements were made for use of a high altitude military helicopter the following day. On May 28, California National Guard helicopter arrived at Siskiyou County airport and loaded four SAR members on board for a high altitude search at 0830. USFS Mountain Ranger Dan Towner hiked from Northgate to the base camp and found it unoccupied and undisturbed at 1024. At 1055 the CNG helicopter reported a possible sighting and landed, offloading two SAR members to investigate. Cain was pronounced dead at the 9,400 foot level of the base of the Bolam Glacier. The body was hoisted aboard and flown out.

It should be noted that Turegun and Cain were on school break from their work as math professors at Oklahoma City Community College and had attempted Mount Shasta earlier. Cain got altitude sickness so they turned back and traveled to Mount Hood in Oregon, but the weather was too bad to climb. They then returned to Mount Shasta for their ill fated climb. (Source: Ron Cloud, with thanks to Sgt. Dave Nickelson—both SAR members)

(Editor's Note: Ron Cloud sent forward two other accounts of incidents on Mount Shasta. Two men (30) and a woman (27) slid 500 feet down the Hotlum/Bolam Route when one of them lost footing on hard ice, fell, and pulled the other two off. They had a cell phone and were able to summon help. In October, a man (50) did the same slide, fracturing a leg and dislocating a shoulder. Taking the time to set up an anchored belay when the glacier turns to ice is time consuming, but so are complicated rescues and healing from serious injuries.)

FALL ON ROCK, INADEQUATE PROTECTION, PROTECTION PULLED OUT, NO HARD HAT
California, Yosemite Valley, Cookie Cliff
On May 26, Stephen Ross (32) was mortally injured in a fall while leading Beverly's Tower, a one-pitch 5.10a route at Cookie Cliff.

Beverly's Tower is reached by scrambling up third-class ledges for about 100 feet. It follows a crack for about ten feet, then continues up a shallow (one to two feet deep) dihedral. There is a 5.10a crux low in the dihedral. Jason Hollinger (23), Ross' partner, anchored himself to a fixed piton in a crack eight feet left of Beverly's Tower and about one foot above his feet. He belayed with a Black Diamond ATC. Meanwhile two friends, Matthew Pearce and Nicola Woolfard, were 10 feet directly below the start of the route on the third class ledges, unroped, looking at other climbs.

Ross climbed 10 feet off the ledge and placed his only protection, a .75 Camalot with an attached 4-in. sling. He said he would move this piece higher as he climbed, then he began to move up into the dihedral. When the Camalot was at his waist he said, "F... me," and fell. Hollinger felt almost no upward force as the Camalot pulled out.

Ross fell past the belay ledge, struck Pearce in the head and back, then struck a ledge with his head and was stopped by the rope after a total fall of 25-35 feet. He probably also struck the rock above Pearce, slowing himself enough that he did not knock Pearce off the wall.

Ross was unconscious and bleeding from head wounds. Hollinger lowered him three or four feet further to a large ledge, where Pearce and Woolfard could help him, then drove to the Arch Rock Entrance Station to notify the NPS. When the first rescuers reached Ross a few minutes after receiving the report, they found him unconscious and not breathing but with a strong pulse. As more rescuers arrived, paramedics stabilized him with an endotracheal tube, oxygen, IV, and spinal immobilization. He was lowered 300 feet down cliffs and scree, and flown by helicopter to Doctor's Medical Center in Modesto. He died the next day from his head injuries.

No one saw the start of Ross's fall (the sun was in Hollinger's eyes), and he did not say anything to Hollinger about the quality of the Camalot placement. The crack at that point was slightly flared; if Ross had brushed the Camalot as he moved up it may have rotated upward and walked closer to the edge of the crack. When we inspected the Camalot, it showed no unusual wear and functioned perfectly. (Source: Mark Fincher, NPS Ranger, Yosemite National Park)

Analysis
According to Ross's partner, Jason Hollinger, Ross was very experienced and led mid 5.11, A4, while Hollinger had been climbing three years and led 5.10c. They had climbed one route together previously. Because this climb starts in steep terrain, the leader faces a serious fall almost immediately and the protection should take this into account. First, the belayer should insist on the leader placing a bombproof directional just off the ledge to establish a direction of pull. Second, the leader should attempt to place solid protection higher, not just a single piece that he/she will move, since it is the only insurance against striking the ledges below. Third, although it apparently did not play a role in this incident, trusting a single fixed piton for a belay, and one that's only a foot off the ledge, is asking for trouble—even if it holds, the belayer may not be stable against a downward pull.

It seems obvious that wearing a helmet might have made all the difference in this situation. All these points may seem obvious after the fact, but all the shortcuts above are common. Maybe the key lesson to remember is that the mistakes were made by a climber with lots of experience - like many of us. (Source: John Dill, NPS Ranger, Yosemite National Park)

PROTECTION PULLED OUT, FALL ON ROCK, NO HARD HAT
California, Tuolumne Meadows, Stately Pleasure Dome
On June 7, 1996, Shannon Meredith, 25, and Dennis Papa decided to climb "West Country", 5.7 PG, on Stately Pleasure Dome in Tuolumne Meadows. Shannon had been climbing for three and a half years and handled nine or ten traditional 5.7 routes. Dennis had been climbing intermittently for ten years and comfortably led 5.8. Shannon led the first pitch, a dihedral on a 70 degree slab allowing only occasional protection in a shallow, somewhat flaring crack. She climbed about 40 feet, placing three nuts. Finding the climbing more difficult than she had expected and fearing that she lacked adequate protection for the rest of the pitch, she decided to retreat. She checked her top piece, a DMM Wallnut, by tugging on it to set it and partially weighting it. Dennis lowered her to the belay, but she decided to climb back up to remove the first two pieces. When she had done so, Dennis again began lowering her off the top piece using his belay device, a figure eight in belay plate mode.

When Shannon was about ten feet above Dennis, the nut pulled. She flipped over and began sliding head first. Dennis tried to grab her as she passed him but she was out of reach. Since there was 70 feet of slack in the system, she continued to slide, going over an overhang and striking her head. Meanwhile, Dennis took up what slack he could by dropping the figure eight and creating a hip belay; he stopped her fall despite being flipped upside down by the impact, and tied her off to the anchor (two Camalots). She did not respond to his calls and he could see that she was hanging from the rope apparently unconscious.

He rappelled to her with their second rope, and called for help to bystanders on the road 400 feet below; they called the NPS dispatcher from the nearby pay phone. Shannon regained consciousness after about 20 minutes, complaining of wrist pain and a headache.

The Yosemite rescue team lowered Shannon to the road three hours after the accident and sent her by ground ambulance to Mammoth Lakes Hospital. She was diagnosed with a moderate concussion, a fractured left wrist, and several abrasions and other soft tissue injuries.

Analysis

Shannon chose a route that she felt was within her ability, but soon discovered that, as the Tuolumne guide book states, route descriptions may be incorrect. She wisely backed off when she found it harder to climb and protect than she expected. Having already lowered off her top piece, she assumed it would hold her weight a second time. However, if she felt she had to test the top piece at all she should have backed it up—only a nut that is visibly trapped in a pocket is secure, for a given direction of pull, and even then you are relying on the integrity of the metal, the sling, and the rock. The guide book warning page—must reading for any climber—states that one should not trust a single piece of fixed protection. That should also include any piece you place yourself.

If you've decided to lower from a single piece, consider either lowering yourself (the line from the belayer runs through a descender on your own harness) or rappelling on both strands. In both cases the force on the piece is roughly half the force on it when the belayer lowers you. This doesn't guarantee security, of course, so keep the belayer in the system (see below).

Dennis's quick thinking in creating a hip belay may have kept Shannon from falling the full 70 feet, but there was a risk of losing control altogether, especially if he had not clipped the rope into a carabiner on his harness. If he had put Shannon on belay with their second rope (or with the unused 90 feet of lead rope) while she climbed and lowered, she would have fallen only 20 feet plus rope stretch.

Their second rope was useful after the fall. Dennis was able to reach Shannon with it and to provide a line for the first ranger to arrive (enabling him to radio information needed by the rescue team and the medical clinic). Dennis had been trained in first aid, but neither of them had discussed or practiced rescue techniques, and neither knew how or where to get help. Could Dennis have gotten his partner to a comfortable spot if no one else were around?

Finally, like Stephen Ross and Joe Presuto (see below), Shannon might have prevented her head injury by wearing a helmet. (Source: Martin Ziebell, John Dill, NPS Rangers, Yosemite National Park)

RAPPEL ERROR, INADEQUATE CLOTHING, HYPOTHERMIA, WEATHER
California, Tuolumne Meadows, Pywiack Dome
On July 23, a powerful thunderstorm swept through Tuolumne Meadows in the early afternoon. My partner and I raced to the top of our route, simulclimbing the last two pitches as the storm bore down on Tenaya Lake. As we reached pavement, the storm cut loose with sheets of rain and violent gusts of wind. On the way to camp, we stopped at the Pywiack Dome pullout to have a look at some climbers who were just topping out on the exit pitches of the Dike Route. We noticed a nearby party on Needle Spoon, a two pitch 5.10a face climb. We checked out the party more closely with binoculars and discovered that they lacked not only raingear, but shirts of any kind (save a jogbra on her).

By now the storm was unleashing infrequent but alarmingly close bolts of lightning. The party began the first rappel from the last anchor station. The woman, who rappelled first, took a long time on rappel, and we began to suspect an epic. As she neared the end of the rappel, which ended on a sloping ledge approximately 200 feet above the ground, I noticed the rap ropes were not even. She stopped at the end of the short side of the rope (which wasn't knotted) and crouched, apparently reaching for the anchors on the first pitch of the Dike Route. As we watched, the rope slipped through her hand and her device and she tumbled approximately eight feet onto the ledge and rolled off. Miraculously, the woman managed to throw an arm onto the ledge to check an inevitable grounder, a move she later attributed to thoughts of her children. Her partner then evened the rope and rapped down. They then tied off the rope for one full length rappel to a point approximately 25 feet above the ground. The woman reached the end of the rappel and was confused as to the best descent and almost incoherent. The two refused dry clothing and dashed for the car where they began to shiver violently in the heat of their vehicle as we spoke of the incident.

Analysis
The party knew of storms in the high country but chose to forego carrying raingear. Lauren Miller, a resident of California, stated that she had been climbing for 13 years. Still, she fell victim to the, "It's the sunny Sierras!" trap. Even on a short route, sodden ropes, violent wind, cold rain, and haste induced by mild hypothermia can be dangerous factors working against the retreating climber. Had the two been faster climbing to the last rappel anchor and rigging the rappels, they would still have been exposed, shirtless, to the cold rain of the thunderstorm for the duration of the descent, which would ordinarily involve two rappels and a fourth class scramble. In their haste to find shelter, the two neglected to locate the rope's center, to knot the ends, and/or to use a "hands free" backup, with almost tragic results. (Source: Frank Carus, ClimbMax Mountain Guides)

RAPPEL ANCHOR FAILURE—INADEQUATE KNOT and PROTECTION,
FALL ON ROCK, HASTE, INEXPERIENCE, SLIGHT HANGOVER
California, Tahquitz Rock
On August 11 around 1100, our party of four climbers in two groups proceeded up the route "The Uneventful" (5.5) at Tahquitz Rock. We did not plan to summit, only rappel

down after completing four pitches. I led the first group up three pitches with no problems. The day was warm, so I decided to remove my helmet while I belayed my partner up. As I took in rope, a loop caught the helmet sitting loose on a rock next to me, whereupon it bounced to the bottom of the route. We continued on one more pitch to where we had lunch. We cut it short when we realized the time (1500) and wanted to get home at a reasonable hour. We set up our first rap anchor by using an older (three years) piece of webbing with a water knot (no backup knots) looped through a rap ring and then around a young but agreeably sturdy pine branch. The first two climbers rapped down to the next station without incident. My partner took a light fall onto a ledge after she had trouble with the rope, but made it down to the station also. I was about halfway down the pitch when I felt slack and looked up to see the rope falling toward me as I was falling backwards. I bounced once on my backside, then turned over, free-falling head first. Since I could see only air between myself and the base, I truly believed I would die. By miraculous fortune, I hit the same two foot wide ledge my partner had and stopped there, six meters below the initial falling point. I was very shaken, but suppressed my panic to maintain the safety of the whole party. I placed an SLCD and wire nut, then rappelled down to my companions. My injuries were not life threatening and I was able to continue the three more raps to the base as well as the walk down to Humber Park. We decided to postpone medical attention until we got home. The injuries turned out to be lacerations and contusions to the chin, lip, knee, and both arms, small fractures to the feet, and a sprained ankle.

Analysis
This was my first multi-pitch experience, but I believed I was within my technical abilities, having led 5.9's and with two years experience. The direct cause of the failure was slippage of the knot due to placement of the rap ring directly on the knot as well as not having backup knots. I questioned the arrangement silently as we placed it, but in our haste, we didn't really scrutinize it. The ring was still attached to the rope after the fall.

But the real causes of the accident were inexperience, not placing redundant bombproof anchors, our haste to get down, and the desire to leave as little protection behind as necessary. In addition, the earlier loss of my helmet was just inexcusable. A light hangover most likely contributed to the lack of attentiveness overall. In retrospect, a more horrendous scenario could have unfolded if the first rappeller had fallen, since he was carrying the rope and there would have been no safe way down for those left behind. After the fall, we left behind double protection at every rap station with intense scrutiny of the systems before anyone ventured out. (Source: Grant Meisenholder)

FALL ON ROCK—FALLING ROCK, INADEQUATE PROTECTION
California, Sequoia National Park, Devil's Crag #1
On September 1, David Dykeman (64) and Herbert Buehler, members of the California Mountaineering Club, were descending from the summit of Devil's Crag #1 (12,400+ feet) about 1400. The weather was clear, with little or no wind. Just below the summit arrete, they set up a short rappel of about 25 feet. Buehler went first while Dykeman waited, unroped, at the top of the rappel. Just when they reached the bottom of the rappel, Buehler heard the noise of a large rockfall, and ducked against the wall for cover. He heard Dykeman cry out, "Oh, no!" When the noise subsided, Buehler looked up at

the top of the pitch. Dykeman was gone. All of the falling rock, and Dykeman's body, had fallen down the northeast side of the peak, a drop of over a thousand feet. Buehler retrieved the rope and climbed down alone to their camp at Rambaud Lake, a difficult descent that required two more rappels. He then continued out for help, arriving at the LeConte backcountry ranger station about 2200, where he found Park Service Ranger George Durkee who radioed news of the accident to Park Headquarters. Park Rangers helicoptered in the next morning and located Dykeman's body, lodged on a snag about midway down the 1,200-foot northeast face. Climbing down from above, and traversing across the face, Rangers Randy Kaufman and Scott Wanek were able to reach Dykeman's body. They hooked his climbing harness to the end of a 50 foot line from a helicopter hovering next to the wall. The difficult operation took four days overall.

Analysis
Devil's Crag #1 has a bad reputation for unstable rock. All the rock on the top of the mountain is badly shattered; big unattached blocks piled one on top of another. It is probable that one or more of the slabs on which Dykeman was standing simply slid suddenly out from under him. The entire upper part of the mountain is one narrow arrete after another, dropping directly off to the steep faces on either side.

Dykeman was a very experienced climber, having made over 500 ascents in the Sierra, as well as others around the world. He had a reputation of being a conservative, safety-conscious climber and leader. This accident probably could have been prevented if Dykeman had been tied in while waiting for his turn to rappel. However, it is possible that the rock collapse would have included his anchor. Additionally, Dykeman, having climbed this peak before, was aware that overly conservative use of ropes has resulted in many parties having to endure uncomfortable bivouacs high on the mountain. (Source: John Inskeep, Sierra Madre Search and Rescue Team)

FALL ON ROCK, INADEQUATE PROTECTION, FAILURE TO FOLLOW ACCEPTED STANDARDS
California, Redmond
On September 21, Travis Hull (28), North American Wilderness Academy school administrator and master wilderness instructor, fell to his death while teaching a beginning rescue class to the NAWA-USA Academy. The USA Academy, composed of teachers and students in grades seven through twelve, were completing the rescue course in preparation for their five week trip to Alaska when the accident occurred.

Travis had just completed a demonstration on the safety of a two point self-protecting system and had yet to hook the ropes into the system. As he extricated himself from the system, he apparently lost contact with how close he was to the edge, stepped back, lost his balance, and fell to his death.

Analysis
Travis was an expert climber and rescue instructor. He was a volunteer coordinator for the Shasta County Search and Rescue and had spent many hours training Sheriff departments, search and rescue groups, and fire departments in vertical and swift water rescue. His contributions to the NAWA program were enormous, and he will be deeply missed by all of us.

As his father, I know he would want me to emphasize one thing: the equipment and the system were safe. The error was his alone as he failed to follow his own and the industry's safety procedures by being too close to the edge without being hooked into the system. As instructors, we work hard to conduct safe situations for youth to (engage in) risk and grow emotionally from that risk. We are oftentimes concerned more with our clients' safety than our own. Don't let your familiarity with your job and your acceptance of the risks momentarily blind you to the inherent dangers. They are always there for each of us. An accidental misstep can have devastating consequences. (Source: David Hull)

FALL ON ROCK, NO HARD HAT
California, Yosemite Valley, Sunnyside Bench
On October 8, Joe Presuto (51) was seriously injured in a fall on the jam crack, 5.9, on Sunnyside Bench.

He protected right off the ground, placed four pieces in the first 40 feet, then ran out the last 30 feet where the difficulty eases off. When he got to the ledge and clipped the bolts, he had plenty of cams and nuts left and elected to go on. He put in a piece just above the bolts and two or three more before reaching the bulge. His partner, Kurt Harms, felt Joe should have protected again before that point, but he was already into the crux, 15 feet above his last piece, and Kurt didn't want to excite him. He could see Joe trying to put in another piece; it looked like he was grappling with his hold and all of a sudden a finger popped out and he said, "I'm going down."

Kurt: "I knew there was maybe 15 feet of runout so Joe was looking at a 30 footer plus rope stretch. I figured I had time to pull up a couple of feet of rope. I got up against the rock. I was belaying with a Sticht Spring Belay Plate in a locking 'biner on my harness. I pulled up slack and felt a light yank and that's apparently when the top piece pulled out. I could feel a little bit of rope stretch beginning so I knew the fall was stopping, but then he hit the ledge with a thud. He bounced and the belay stopped him from rolling off the ledge. There was weight on my rope after he stopped falling.

"I called out to him, 'Joe!, Joe!' for 20-30 seconds and got no answer. Then I stood there holding the rope, yelling for help for two or three minutes until someone responded. [*The route is only 200 feet from a popular tourist trail near Yosemite Village—Ed.*] I knew I needed to tie him off, but my anchor was a single piece placed for an upward pull, so first I put in two pieces to oppose it. Since I didn't have his full weight, I was able to hold on to the rope on his side of the belay with my left hand; I fed some rope through the plate to get slack on his side and tied him off.

"Once I got out of the belay I went up the talus to the right a bit so I could communicate with him better. I told him, 'Joe, wake up, wake up!' Blood was trickling down the rock, all the way to the ground. He sat up and started moving around, and asked me, 'Who are you?' I said, 'It's me, Kurt. Check yourself, run your hands through your hair, see where you're bleeding.' He was doing it. At that point he started to get up and I thought about lowering him, but I didn't trust the pieces still above him. I said, 'Help is coming, so stay where you are.'"

About that time the rescue team began arriving. Two paramedics and other rescuers climbed the first pitch, to find Joe conscious but confused, and bleeding from head wounds. They gave him oxygen, stabilized his spine, packaged him in a litter and lowered him to the ground. Two hours after his fall he was flown to Doctor's Medical Center in Modesto.

The diagnosis: A fractured skull on the right side; damage to facial nerves; perforated right eardrum; bone chips in the right elbow; severe bruises on the right hip and ligament damage in the right ankle. He has recovered from most of his injuries, but his short-term memory is worse than before the accident, and he remembers nothing of the climb nor of the following 10 days.

Analysis

Presuto had followed his partner, Kurt Harms, for the first two seasons as he developed protection skills and was now comfortably leading 5.7 and 5.8, with an occasional 5.9 and 5.10. He had been climbing for the past three years, but he'd never taken a leader fall.

This was their first climbing trip since July, so they picked the jam crack as a well-protected warm-up. A 70-foot 5.7 crack ends at a ledge with a bolt anchor, followed by another 70-foot crack with a 5.8-5.9 crux at a bulge. The climb can be done as either one full pitch or two short ones. Kurt had led the route before but Joe was new to it; this was his lead and he had the option to stop halfway or continue.

The leader: It's easy to miscalculate your protection. Joe knew better, yet he found himself at an insecure stance, well above the critical piece protecting him from hitting the ledge, probably wishing he had backed it up when he had had the chance. (The crack allows several options just below the crux.) Here's another way to look at it: If you wouldn't rappel on that single piece, would you lead with it being your only protection against a ground fall? Fairly new leaders, like Joe, should sew up those pitches, for practice if nothing else. Finally, the obvious: wearing a helmet may be a headache, but that's all Joe might have suffered, had he worn one.

The belayer: As Kurt discovered, the belay anchor serves both to keep the belayer in place and to tie off an injured partner; after the fall is not the best time to be beefing it up. He felt his single upward piece was solid but, without an opposing counterpart right from the start, he was risking an encounter with Murphy's Law. Second, if Joe had been hanging in space Kurt would have found it more difficult to tie him off as he did. It's easier and safer to tie a Prusik hitch on the loaded rope after the fall and clip the hitch to the anchor; that way, Joe is held by the belay device until he's clipped in.

Medical care: Really serious external bleeding is rare— scalp wounds look horrible but usually stop bleeding by themselves, while broken necks or other life-threatening unstable injuries are more common. So Joe was better off lying still than moving around. That's also why lowering Joe to the ground before he was stabilized and packaged, would be dangerous, even if Kurt trusted Joe's protection. An exception: The patient is hanging on the rope, getting worse from the harness or the injuries and rescuers won't get there in time. (Source: John Dill, NPS Ranger, Yosemite National Park)

BOLT PULLED OUT—BADLY SET, FALL ON ROCK
California, Joshua Tree National Park, Indian Cove

Having led aid climbs (some solo, and all without incident) during the long Thanksgiving weekend, including the A4's Rurp Romp and Lost Lid ("New wave" A2+ or A3) on Beaver Boulder, I (40) turned my attention toward another objective for a short day of fun. While leading a supposed A1 bolt ladder, Unknown Highway, on Willit Slab in

Indian Cove, a bolt on the lower part of the pitch pulled out under body weight (with no outward pull), precipitating a fall of eight to ten feet. The bolt immediately below (at the back of a wide ledge) had been extended with a single-length runner to decrease rope drag, and bolts lower on the route had been extended with short, quick draw slings for the same reason. During the fall, a small shelf below my feet ejected me out past the ledge below (probably preventing further injury), and as I was caught by the belay, my right foot struck a small bulge near the third bolt on the route, causing a traumatic inversion injury. Realizing a probable fracture, I was lowered to the ground, taped, splinted and then evacuated to the High Desert Hospital in Joshua Tree for further treatment. The first aid and evacuation was executed by my partner and a nearby friend, a member of the So Cal Mountaineers' Association. No request was made of any Park Ranger, JOSAR or paramedic staff members. The staff in the very busy Emergency Department took X-rays that indicated a severe sprain and a minor fracture. I was given an elastic bandage, a pair of crutches, copies of the X-rays, and instructions to get further evaluation and treatment from my own doctor.

Analysis
The bolt that pulled out was a 1/4" by 1" Rawl screw top. I recognized that it was a bad stubby bolt, in that I could see the split portion of the shank when I placed a hanger on it. The hole seemed to be intact, with no evidence of having been broken or otherwise compromised. I tightened the nut by hand. But after weighting the aiders (and unclipping aiders from the bolt below), it pulled out. (Source: Jerry Cox.)

(Editor's Note: Joshua Tree National Park personnel were not able to provide incident reports in time for publication due to constraints of budget and other resources. One unusual California accident that didn't make it into the statistics involved three 17 year old young men who were rappelling 150 feet from an electrical tower in Camarillo, CA. They were about ready to go home. The last to rappel was Michael Halsell. The winds had picked up to 30 mph. His two friends reported hearing a loud explosion and two pops, looked up and saw Halsell on fire. He was rescued by Ventura County Fire Engineer David Pumphrey and Captain Scott Hall. He died two weeks later from complications resulting from the burns that covered 80 percent of his body. Ken Gerry submitted this report.)

AVALANCHE, FAILURE TO FOLLOW ADVICE, INADEQUATE EQUIPMENT, POOR POSITION, INEXPERIENCE
Colorado, Pyramid Peak
On January 28, a party of four climbers headed up Maroon Creek Road south of Aspen during a heavy avalanche cycle, following a major snow storm. The road is not plowed during the winter, but is used by a commercial snowmobile operation. Due to the avalanche danger, snowmobilers were not using the road at the time; it is exposed to numerous avalanche runouts. The climbing party encountered an employee of the snowmobile operation who advised them of the avalanche hazard. On the group's approach to 14,018-foot Pyramid Peak the climbers snowshoed over several large, fresh avalanche debris piles lying across the road. After snowshoeing in approximately eight miles, the party passed from the road into the Snowmass-Maroon Bells Wilderness and began an ascent

of the steep, northwest facing side of the glacial valley, toward the amphitheater at the base of the north face of the peak. This ascent was begun in darkness around 1930. Partway up the valley's side, the climbers, still in snowshoes, triggered an avalanche estimated to be 300 feet wide with a three-foot deep crown. The avalanche traveled approximately 1,400 vertical feet to the valley floor, carrying one member of the team over a cliff. The other climbers carried no shovels or avalanche beacons and were not able to locate the lost climber. The buried body of the climber was located by searchers three weeks later.

Analysis
These climbers were from southern Europe and had experience climbing in the Alps. During discussions with the surviving climbers, rescuers learned the group assumed that Colorado's alpine snowpack would behave in the more stable manner they were accustomed to encountering in the maritime climate of the southern Alps. Consequently, they had discounted the evidence of avalanche instability around them, and the verbal warning they had received. They had been warned by acquaintances in Denver to avoid this peak, but their lack of understanding of the dynamics of objective winter hazard in the region, combined with their determination to climb the peak despite evidence indicating they should not proceed, suggest that the result may not have been easily prevented. Although the team carried no avalanche rescue equipment, doing so probably would have made no difference to the deceased member, who apparently died from multiple trauma suffered during the slide. (Source: From Mountain Rescue- Aspen, Inc., compiled by Hal Clifford)

(Editor's Note: While these victims were snowshoeing as opposed to climbing, the conditions encountered required mountaineering expertise.)

FALL ON ROCK, PROTECTION PULLED OUT
Colorado, Rocky Mountain National Park, The Book
On May 6, at 1900, Jorge Arias (40) was leading the final pitch of Cheap Date III, 5.10b, on The Book. Arias fell 20 feet from a point about 50 feet from the top of the climb and ten feet from the crux. As he fell, one piece of protection pulled out. Arias impacted the lateral aspect of his right thigh against the rock and sustained a fracture of the right femur. His partners, Chris Stewart and Mark Hammond, attempted to evacuate Arias by lowering him back to the belay ledge and then raising him to the top of the climb. Due to the obvious severity of the injury and the resultant pain, Stewart and Hammond aborted the remainder of their planned evacuation after three hours, leaving Arias comfortable at the top of the route while they descended the east gully in the dark. A park service rescue crew responded, stabilized Arias, and lowered him a total of 1,200 feet, including a 650 foot vertical litter lowering.

Analysis
Arias was an experienced rock climber with international climbs to his credit. The fall took him by surprise as he was not yet at the crux; hence the poor landing against the hip. More frequently climbers anticipate their falls, and are able to assume an injury-defensive position facing the cliff right side up, with feet impacting against the cliff with

knees slightly bent to absorb some of the impact energy that would be totally borne by the ankles. Another recurrent theme in recent years with the popularity of bolt-protected routes is the failure of either mechanical or non-mechanical chocks. Thoroughly understand and practice using these devices before committing your life to them on a traditional lead!

Partners Stewart and Hammond put forth a very determined effort in their attempts to evacuate Arias. However, their decision to abort the evacuation when they realized the serious nature of Arias' injuries was even more significant to Arias' survival, as a fractured femur injury, if not stabilized, may become fatally complicated if loose bone internally shifts and ruptures major arteries. (Source: Jim Detterline, Longs Peak Supervisory Climbing Ranger)

RAPPEL ERROR—DID NOT SECURE RAPPEL ANCHOR SLING
Colorado, Eldorado Canyon State Park
On May 6, after belaying his partners down a 20 to 30 foot cliff, the victim (39) fell about 30 feet while rappelling. A Ranger found a red sling girth hitched around a tree with no knot in it. Apparently the victim placed the red sling around the tree and added a descending ring, but did not securely tie off the sling. The descending ring, rappelling device and locking carabiner were all securely attached to the victim.

Analysis
Know the appropriate knots to use. And always double check them. (Source: J. W. Wilder, Park Ranger)

FALL ON ROCK, PROTECTION PULLED OUT
Colorado, Eldorado Canyon State Park, Kloof
On May 22, the victim (29) was leading a climb on the route called Kloof on the west ridge. He was about 30 feet off the ground when he was unable to complete a move. He fell, pulling out his only piece of protection.

Analysis
Because of the angle of the rock face, the protection would not hold properly. Thought needs to be given to the angle of the rock in relationship to the angle if one was to fall and the force that the fall would place on the protection. (Source: J. W. Wilder, Park Ranger)

FALL ON WET ROCK, PLACED INADEQUATE PROTECTION, NO HARD HAT
Colorado, Eldorado Canyon State Park, Ruper
On May 27, the victim (29) was leading Ruper when he fell. In his own words: "Water was seeping over the saddle, covering most of the last pitch. I tried to skirt the water (off-route) but ran out of real estate. While traversing the wet section, I slipped and fell. I hit my head almost immediately (no helmet) and was knocked unconscious. Total fall was 60 feet (run out—it even mentions this in the guide book). Two other parties assisted my partner in rescuing me. My injuries: serious abrasions, minor lacerations, concussion, basilar skull fracture. (Source: Brooke Hoyer)

FALL ON ROCK, PROTECTION PULLED OUT
Colorado, Eldorado Canyon State Park, Bastille Crack

On June 1, the victim (28) climbed about 30 feet up the Bastille Crack, slipped while making a traverse, and while falling pulled out his only piece of protection and consequently hit the ground.

(Editor's Note: Protection pulling out—or simply inadequate protection—is very common in this climbing area.)

FALL ON ROCK, HELMET NOT SECURED PROPERLY
Colorado, Boulder, First Flat Iron

It was June 8. We had been working hard the last few months, warming up for our annual trip to Chamonix. We had decided to have an easy day on the First Flatiron. The easiest route on the formation is Bakers Way. After a 40 foot section of steep 5.4, the route is basically a hike until it intersects with the other east face routes above Junction Knob. Since the first pitch was the only climbing on the route and since 5.4 is well below what Debbi has been leading, she took the lead. The first pitch is the only interesting part of the route until the North Arrete. We put on our helmets. Hardly anyone we see climbing on the Flatirons wears them. We do. Because it was going to be a hot day, Debbi put a bandanna visor under hers so that it was not completely snug. She'll never do that again. Had it been snug, her head injuries would have been much less severe. She began the little 40-foot head wall. She got up to the first step and seemed a bit unsure but moved on up anyway. I considered calling her back and leading it myself, but decided to let her work it out. The first opportunity for protection was about 20 feet off the deck. She had made two steps and was standing on the edge of her right shoe (I had told her not to do this) when it let go. I saw nothing that looked like an attempt to catch herself with hands or feet. For an instant, she had rolled sideways and started down the rock and out of sight. My recollection is in slow motion with a feeling of disbelief both at the fall itself and at her not appearing to fight it. The angle of the fall and the lack of protection meant that there was a lot of rope out. So, I started immediately to reel in rope hand over hand. I heard rustling but no sounds from her as she fell. When the rope finally came taut, it burned through my hands for a few feet; then, silence.

Without untying, I ran down to where she was lying, about 30 feet below me. In all, it seemed that she fell about 50 feet. I began screaming for help and rescue. She was lying on her left side, head down. She was unconscious. The sound of her breathing indicated an obstruction. My first thought was that her orthodontic plate was in the air passage. Her face was a mass of blood and I could see a very large knot forming on the right side of her forehead and extending back under her helmet which had been pushed back. Without thinking about possible neck injuries (big mistake), I cradled her head and began trying to open her mouth to remove the orthodontic plate. She became so animated later on that it's questionable whether I could have prevented her from moving if I had tried. Her jaw was clenched and it took me several minutes to open her mouth and get the plate out. I had visions of losing a finger in the process. By the time I got it out, she had started to come around. It turns out that the obstructed breathing was a result of nose and facial blows.

At this point, a medical student from Denver GH showed up along with two hikers. The hikers helped gather up the gear and the medical student and I worked with Debbi to get her out up to the trail. Her pupillary reflexes were uniform but she was essentially oblivious. There were no indentations in the skull and no blood in her ears. We got her out of her harness and left the gear for the hikers to collect. Between us, myself and the medical student, we got her to walk up the gully to the trail and down the trail to just below the rock steps, probably 100 yards in all. The fact that she could walk and actually negotiated the rock steps is absolutely amazing! I have no exact idea of the elapsed time for all this, but it probably took nearly half an hour, maybe longer.

An EMT crew arrived and started administering IV and oxygen. She fought the oxygen nostril feed and the mask. No doubt the nostril feed was ineffectual anyway since her nose was completely clogged with blood. It wasn't until she was in the Stokes and immobilized that we could keep the oxygen on her. The Rocky Mountain Rescue team showed up with the Stokes and an inflatable immobilization bag. Debbi managed to stand up and walk over to the Stokes and lie down. But then, as she was strapped in, she became increasingly more combative. Since she was face up, sunshine was a nuisance, so I put her sun glasses on her. This seemed to help. Because it was a warm day, her combativeness increased every time she was in the direct sun. So, I got the crew to adopt the practice of making sure the rest stops were in the shade. Still, whenever we stopped, Debbi became restive. Good for her! She continued to tell me to JUST DO IT! I never found out what she wanted. I suppose it was her way of fighting the confusion and pain. This in itself was very encouraging.

The rescue team wanted to lower the Stokes down the rock spur that the rock steps go through. This meant hauling the Stokes back up the steps about fifty feet. We had actually walked Debbi too far down the trail. So, after attaching a goldline rope to the Stokes for belay purposes, we helped to raise it to the top of the rock spur and the rescue team took over. I gathered up our gear and started down the trail. At this point, the medical student pointed out that I had sustained a pretty severe rope burn on my right hand. He had a small first aid kit, so I put a piece of gauze on and went on, handling the rope on the back belay, etc. It wasn't until late Sunday while in the ICU that one of the ICU staff noticed it and I actually got it dressed. By then it had gotten close to being a real problem. I guess the belay must have helped a bit after all if the severity of the wound is any indication of the force absorbed.

Because of the trail's circuitous route, we arrived at the bottom of the rock spur (actually the gully east of it) where it crosses the switchbacks just as the team and the Stokes arrived. At this point, the lowering was over and the belayed carry stage commenced. Six people supported the Stokes and someone managed the IV. I took the rope at the front near Debbi's head; numerous others assisted in providing a back belay for the Stokes. All the way down the hill, Debbi protested. She kept cursing, demanding that we let her stand up, and screaming. Actually, in order to keep some kind of link to her consciousness, I used this behavior. I instructed her to scream when I told her to. So, all the way to the ambulance, I'd say, "Scream," and she would. I didn't know she had that kind of volume! She also never indicated any nausea or dizziness... usually a good sign with a head injury. Once we had crossed the talus fields, a fat tire was attached to the bottom of the Stokes so that it could be rolled. From there, the trip to Blue Bell parking lot took fewer than five minutes.

The ambulance left and I was taken in one of the Ranger vehicles directly to Boulder Community Hospital, gear and all. About 1500, a Dr. Bowles, neurosurgeon, came out and said that the CT scan was negative: no subdural hematoma, the biggest worry. Bad news was that Debbi had a skull fracture and a broken clavicle (three pieces) and scapula.

We later found out she had broken her wrist and cracked her right orbit, too. One week later, she was home and looking forward to a near complete recovery, albeit a lengthy one.

Analysis
The fall should never have occurred. When I saw uncertainty, I should have pulled Debbi off the pitch and led it myself. It probably would have been more effective if I had taken up the slack by running headlong up the hill from the belay and let the belay device catch the fall. The hand over hand technique didn't help much.

Helmets are made to be worn snug to the cranium, not "sort of on top of the head." Wearing a bandanna or other paraphernalia under a helmet just means that it can be knocked out of place when you most need it.

I should NEVER have moved Debbi without immobilizing her spinal column. We were lucky. The "shout line" down the mountain definitely works. People know how to pass along the alarm.

Rocky Mountain Rescue will be getting some more donations. (Source: G. N. Jones)

(Editor's Note: The reporter of this incident gives us a good narrative description of the aftermath. However, he raises a question in the opening of his analysis. How many of us would "pull" our partner off if he/she seemed hesitant? What is a reasonable way to resolve such an issue?)

FALL ON ROCK, INADEQUATE (NO) BELAY, MISCOMMUNICATION
Colorado, Eldorado Canyon State Park, Wind Tower
On June 30, a climber (16) fell 15 feet onto a rock ledge on Wind Tower. She thought she was being protected by the top rope. The rope went from her belayer (41) through the victim's harness. The belayer did not have her on belay. Consequently, she had no protection when she fell. (Source: J. W. Wilder, Park Ranger)

FALL ON SNOW, UNABLE TO PLACE PROTECTION, POOR POSITION
Colorado, Mount Powell, Northwest Couloir
On July 6, W. H. (m. 26) and K. D. (f. 30) decided to climb unroped because of lack of available protection and soft snow unable to hold snow flukes or stakes. At the top of the snowfield, footing gave way, K. D. tumbled down 1,000 feet of Hourglass Couloir, colliding with rock walls of a narrow chute. W. H. climbed down to K.D., while other members of the party left the field for a 911 call. K. D. was conscious with obvious fracture of the upper extremities. SAR responded with 14 members, resulting in Flight for Life evacuation. (Source: Summit County Search and Rescue)

FALL ON ROCK, PLACED INADEQUATE PROTECTION, EXCEEDING ABILITIES
Colorado, Rocky Mountain National Park, Bookmark
On July 11, at 1145, Shanna M. Ryan (26) was climbing Backflip (II 5.9), the first pitch on the Bookmark, when she took a 20 foot lead fall. She had been placing protection at the time of the fall, but suddenly slipped and yelled, "Falling." When she swung into the view of belayer Tye Gribb, Ryan was upside down and unresponsive. Despite wearing a

helmet, Ryan had sustained a head injury which included a laceration four inches from the base of the skull which was three to four inches long and to the bone, as well as a concussion. Ryan became responsive upon regaining consciousness one minute later, and was lowered to the ground at her request. A response by Rocky Mountain National Park rangers and Estes Park Medical Center crew effected a ground evacuation to Estes Park Medical Center.

Analysis
Investigating ranger Karl Pearson concluded that, "Ryan was prepared for the climb but either failed to protect it adequately or was climbing beyond her capabilities." There was no further information on what type of helmet Ryan was wearing, but it is possible that the helmet spared her from even further injury. As a final consideration, climbers need to choose as comfortable a stance as possible when placing protection, as this moment can be one of the most vulnerable to falls due to the demands beyond mere physical climbing which are placed on the leader. (Source: Jim Detterline, Longs Peak Supervisory Climbing Ranger)

FALL ON SNOW—LOSS OF CONTROL—VOLUNTARY GLISSADE
Colorado, Rocky Mountain National Park, Longs Peak
On July 14, at 1045, Nathan Dick (51) lost control while glissading near the top of Lamb's Slide on Longs Peak shortly after he had completed its ascent. He slid all the way (approximately 1,000 feet) down and out of control to impact the rocks at the base of Lamb's Slide. Dick had attempted to self-arrest on the hard packed snow surface but was unsuccessful. Instead, he impaled himself in the neck with his ice ax, lacerating his right subclavian artery. Dick also sustained various injuries to left hip, right clavicle, right elbow, neck and ulnar nerve. His fall was witnessed by several climbers who immediately came to his aid and thus saved his life. Vladmir Farkash, in particular, was able to significantly slow the arterial bleeding with direct pressure until relieved by RMNP paramedic climbing ranger Mike Pratt. A Rocky Mountain Rescue volunteer found Dick's cell phone in his pocket, and used it to immediately start the RMNP rescue team on a response.

Analysis
Since the epic 1871 uncontrolled descent of Lamb's Slide by Rev. Elkannah Lamb, the accident has been repeated continually with results varying greatly from no injury to death. Nathan Dick has been very grateful to both climbers and park rescuers for preventing him from crossing that thin line to the latter category. Lamb's Slide becomes hard-surfaced and then icy starting about mid-July every summer. The icy areas usually start about one third up this couloir and in midsummer may be limited to a short section. Thus it is instructive to observe conditions carefully while ascending so that you are aware of such hazards for the descent. Options to consider in lieu of glissading Lamb's Slide include: (1) down climbing Lamb's Slide; (2) rappelling from rock walls on the right moat; (3) topping out to the left and descending the Loft; and (4) scrambling down Glacier Ridge. The evacuation of Nathan Dick to proper hospital care is noteworthy. An Aerostar medical helicopter was unable to reach Mills Glacier due to winds but did shuttle rescue personnel and supplies. Ranger Dan Ostrowski led a litter team through four 200 foot lowers, including three on ice and snow and one on scree. Ranger Scott

Hall ran up to Chasm Lake in approximately 45 minutes carrying a 65 pound raft on his back. Dick was floated across Chasm Lake by the "Long's Peak Navy" to a waiting Aerostar. (Source: Jim Detterline, Longs Peak Supervisory Climbing Ranger)

FALL ON SNOW, UNROPED, POOR POSITION
Colorado, Mount Sneffles

(Following is a letter from Adam Beal [early 20's] to a friend.)
Our plan was to set up a base camp on Sunday, and then do a technical ascent of Mount Sneffles on June 24. The climb up Mount Sneffles (14,000 feet) had us crossing talus, snow, ice and rock. The climb was easy but committing, seven pitches and about 1,000 feet of 5.1 to 5.5 climbing. At the end of the climb we reached a couloir that we planned to climb the final 100 to 200 feet to the summit on. After realizing that it was time to descend whether or not we could summit, I decided to check the couloir as a possible descent route. I walked about 30 feet out onto the snow, and decided against glissading down because of the softness and 45 or 50 degree grade. Then I slipped. I didn't have crampons on my feet for traction, nor did I have a rope on (after being roped for about eight hours that day). I tried a few times to self-arrest with my ice ax, but the snow was just too soft. I was at the mercy of the mountain, and probably moved 30 to 50 mph down the snow as I rammed into boulders and the walls of the couloir on my way down. When I finally stopped around 1,500 feet lower than I had started, I was amazingly lucky to be alive. I landed at the base of the snow on a rocky talus slope.

So there I was, alone and badly injured at 13,000 feet. I had a right wrist that had been broken in three or four places, and my formerly white climbing helmet was now red from the trauma to my face. I had a deep cut under my left eyebrow, the inside of my lower lip was badly cut and my upper lip was ripped clean through with a gash over an inch long. I was disoriented but still quite conscious. I immediately grabbed my first aid kit from my pack, which luckily was still attached to my back, and splinted my wrist with a splint and an ace bandage. Then I knew that it was time to descend back to base camp, 2,000 feet and one to two miles away. I left my pack and helmet, unable to carry them, and started off. I yelled for my partner Geoff or to anyone else who could hear me, but I heard no reply. It was now almost dark, and not having the strength to descend on foot, I started sliding down on my butt. The slope here was very mild, so I was at least safe from another fall. After two hours of sliding and yelling, I finally heard Geoff yelling back to me and could faintly see his headlamp in the darkness. Since I had forgotten my headlamp in my pack, I had to yell to him until he reached me.

Geoff had slowly cut footsteps for himself as he descended on foot the very way that I had slid. After assessing my injuries, he tried to help me to my feet to get to base camp. I was still unable to walk, so we started sliding down together, my legs and arms wrapped around Geoff. After a few minutes, I realized that I could go no further, so Geoff left me for our base camp to get sleeping bags. As he left, he warned me not to fall asleep. With the incredible amount of pain in my wrist, that seemed easy.

Geoff returned about one to one and a half hours later with our bags and the good news that he'd run into some other people camped near us. They left immediately to go get help even though it was probably near 2300 and it was three or four miles to the trailhead and another 30 to 60 minutes to a phone. My friend stayed by my side as I warmed in both of our bags for a while. After a short time I was able to give him back his bag, but he stayed awake all night to watch over me. Since I had forgotten to grab any pain pills from my first aid kit, I was in an amazing amount of pain and was only able to sleep for a few minutes at a time.

Almost at the crack of dawn, three people on the mountain rescue team arrived where we were around 12,500 feet. By this time, my eyes were so swollen shut that I couldn't see any of my rescuers. After stabilizing my neck and placing me into a Stokes litter, they called for a helicopter to airlift me out. Thirty minutes in the helicopter got me to a hospital in Montrose. Luckily, I was given a good dose of morphine for pain, and slept for the entire airlift. I woke up in the emergency room where they proceeded to cut all of my expensive outdoor clothes off my body with trauma shears. My face was sewn up in three places by a plastic surgeon and then I was taken to surgery for the wrist. I woke up with four pins in my wrist.

I spent two and a half days in the hospital. While I was there, I realized that I had lost half of one of my front upper teeth (to be repaired over the next few weeks with a root canal, cap and crown) and that my entire face had been abraded by the snow so badly that it was almost completely scabbed over. I couldn't eat solid food for almost a week afterwards.

My parents flew me back to Michigan on Thursday afternoon. I met my mom and brother at Detroit Metro, and they didn't recognize me at first. When they both realized who I was, they started… crying. It sucked. And here I've been ever since.

FALL ON ROCK—ROCK FOOTHOLD CAME OFF, FAILURE TO TEST HOLD, PROTECTION PULLED OUT
Colorado, Rocky Mountain National Park, Spearhead

On July 23, at 1030, Michael Munsch (34) was leading the fourth pitch (5.6) on the Sykes Sickle route (III 5.9+) on Spearhead. He climbed 20 feet above the belay ledge, placed a "marginal" piece of protection, and continued another five to ten feet. At this point, Munsch stepped on a loose rock which gave way. Munsch fell, the marginal piece of protection failed, and he impacted on the ledge with belayer David T. Many. Munsch sustained fractures of both ankles and soft tissue injury to his right elbow. Many lowered Munsch three pitches to the ground, and then went for assistance to park ranger Dave McKee at Black Lake. Munsch's injuries were stabilized and he was evacuated by Flight for Life helicopter from the base of the climb.

Analysis

Spearhead and its most traveled routes such as Sykes Sickle have a well-deserved reputation for sound and solid quartz monzonite rock. However, even the best alpine rock is subject to freeze-thaw effects, where water creeps behind cracks, pushes a rock when it turns to ice at night and expands, and thus loosens rocks to become climbers' traps. The pitch Munsch fell on was moderate; much below his leading standards, and was typical of alpine rock in that the lower-angled pitches are those most subject to freeze-thaw effects. Treat alpine rock like desert rock, testing or gradually weighting holds. Place the best protection possible at regular intervals despite the easiness of the climbing.

Munsch did an excellent job of landing correctly (on his feet) after his fall, and he was wearing a helmet, but the distance and hard surface factors were too significant to avoid injury. Many is to be commended for his excellent and efficient handling of a severely-injured partner on a three pitch evacuation, and for his prompt summoning of the emergency medical system. (Source: Jim Detterline, Longs Peak Supervisory Climbing Ranger)

STRANDED, UNABLE TO ROUTE-FIND, INADEQUATE CLOTHING AND EQUIPMENT, WEATHER, DARKNESS, EXCEEDING ABILITIES
Colorado, Rocky Mountain National Park, The Book

On July 28, James Griffith (31), Adam Seelig (24) and Erv Wolf were benighted and stranded 100 feet from the top of The Book formation on Lumpy Ridge. They had been attempting the J Crack (IV 5.10) but were unable to figure out the Cave Exit. When the sun set and rain began to fall, they began to yell for help from their perch on the east edge of Fang Ledge. MacGregor Ranch manager Eric Adams and his young son heard the yells of the stranded climbers, and reported the incident to Rocky Mountain National Park. Park rangers responded to the scene and rappelled to the stranded climbers. Then they assisted the climbers in rappelling 450 feet to the base of The Book formation.

Analysis

A number of small errors contributed to this serious situation. The party had a late start (1545) from the trailhead two miles away. Dangerous thunder showers often move suddenly into the area at this time of day. They did not start climbing until 1715 and were moving too slowly with a cumbersome party of three persons. When it became dark at 2030, none of the climbers had headlamps. It began to storm a short time later. None of the climbers had rain gear. In fact, they did not have basic survival gear of warm clothing, water, food, or proper rappel gear, and they were all dressed lightly in shorts and t-shirts, which contributed to their hypothermia.

They stated that they were more used to bolt-protected sport routes on short cliffs and rock gymnasiums. That type of background does not prepare climbers for descents involving multiple rappels, proper placement of chocks and camming devices, and route-finding. (Source: Jim Detterline, Longs Peak Supervisory Climbing Ranger)

FALL ON SNOW, INADEQUATE EQUIPMENT, CLIMBING ALONE
Colorado, Rocky Mountain National Park, Mount Alice

On August 29, David Ingersoll (40) left the Wild Basin Trailhead alone to check out possible routes on the East face of Mount Alice. Ingersoll scrambled part way up the Central Ramp Route (III 5.7, A2), but decided to descend after it began to rain. He scrambled down to a snowfield just left of the center of the East face, and began descending the snowfield. At 1415 while descending, Ingersoll lost his footing when he reached an icy area of the mostly soft snowfield. He was wearing tennis shoes and did not have an ice ax. Unable to self-arrest, he slid 150 feet at a high rate of speed and impacted on rocks, fracturing his pelvis in four places.

Ingersoll's friend Kelly Price called RMNP dispatch on August 30 at 0830 to report that Ingersoll was overdue somewhere in the park, but that she did not know what his plans were. A general trailhead check of the park found Ingersoll's vehicle at 0930, and Ingersoll was found at 1755.

Analysis

Investigating Ranger Karl Pearson pointed to three factors that contributed to Ingersoll's accident and the resulting SAR efforts. He was alone, he failed to tell anyone where he was going, which complicated efforts to find him, and he descended a snowfield without crampons and ice ax. In the investigator's opinion, the above mistakes could have cost Ingersoll his life. When Ingersoll was discovered by RMNP Ranger/searcher Gregg

Tinkham, he was in the initial stages of hypothermia. Ingersoll said that he didn't think he would have survived another night out. It was therefore fortunate that Tinkham found him before dark and was able to have a helicopter fly him out immediately to advanced medical care at a hospital. (Source: Jim Detterline, Longs Peak Supervisory Climbing Ranger)

FALL ON ROCK, PROTECTION PULLED OUT, NO HARD HAT
Colorado, Boulder Canyon, Dome Rock

On September 25, I was climbing with a friend in Boulder Canyon on Gorilla's Delight (5.9+) on Dome Rock. We originally intended to climb in Eldorado Canyon, but it was raining there and was clear to the north, and the granite of Boulder Canyon beckoned. Doug had led the climb a few weeks before, and he bestowed on me the honor of the sharp end. I had been climbing well all summer, and had redpointed a number of 5.10 *and* 5.11 routes, both traditional and sport. I felt completely comfortable on 9+, and looked forward to a pleasant day in the sun. I was so relaxed about the climb that I left my helmet in my pack at the base. "A nice casual day on some classic pitches, and a beer at the car," I thought to myself as we racked up.

I had forgotten that years ago I had read Henry Barber's description of his experience on Gorilla's Delight in Bob Godfrey's book, *Climb* (Alpine Press Publishing, Boulder, Colorado, 1977, currently out of print). Barber was visiting Colorado in 1973 and a friend told him that nobody had soloed the climb. Since it was "only 5.9," Barber decided to free solo it. Godfrey described Barber's solo this way: "I was feeling good at the time. The first crack went real smoothly. I was feeling flowing and really hyped up, kind of in a music mood." At the top of the first crack, he traversed right and laybacked up a flake, which, as the guidebook had stated, was 5.7. From good holds at the top of the flake, he was able to reach around a corner and could see a smooth, steep slab of granite leading upwards. The guidebook had called the slab 5.7 or 5.8. "There should be some nice fat holds up here," thought Henry to himself. At this point he was some 150 feet above the ground. Holding on to the layback crack with his left hand, his right hand explored the surface of the slab for holds, but there were none to be found.

Henry began to sweat. Reversing the layback crack, he moved back down to a resting place and took stock of the situation. "5.7 or 5.8 slabs? I must be missing something." Henry found himself poised on minute ripples in the smooth granite, contemplating a 150 foot fall to the ground. "It's the nearest I've ever come to buying it," he recalls.

Henry made it, by the skin of his teeth. It must have been quite a rush. I faced the same moves, but I was clipped to five pieces by the time I reached the friction slab section above the layback crack. I wasn't panicked about falling off the thin slab move, because I had a quadcam at my feet, and a medium nut four feet below that. I moved up, saw how thin the right foot smear was going to be, and backed down to rest and think about the sequence. Feeling confident, I moved up again, forgot the sequence I had planned, and fell prey to the temptation of leaning in and reaching for a secure-looking finger crack with my left hand. The result was predictable: my right foot unweighted and smeared off the thin slab. I was airborne.

I heard the quadcam and the stopper rip out as I fell past, and my next memory is of my right shoulder, upper back, and the back of my head smashing into the sloping ledge 15 feet below. There was a kind of an electric flashing sensation when I hit my head that hard, and after the electric flash, I have vague memories of a pleasant, dreamlike state. No pain, completely relaxed, very restful, a kind of light sleep. While I was dreaming, I fell another 15 feet or so.

As I came to I remember briefly thinking that I was in bed at home. I was very disappointed to find that instead of being next to my warm wife, I was hanging upside down over a hundred feet of air, ten feet below my belayer. Blood dripped from my forehead and nose. I felt more drowsy than afraid. Mohammed Ali wrote a perfect description (in his book *The Greatest*) of the quasi-unconscious state that follows a severe punch to the head. In his fights with Joe Frazier he spent some time nearly unconscious. He says it's like being in a little dark room with bats flying around, birds singing, and ghostlike figures fading in and out of view. While I was in that little room I noticed that I could not breathe. The fall had slammed every molecule of air out of my lungs, and the muscles that control the intake of breath were traumatized and not inclined to contract. Shit, oh dear, I thought, and made horrible groaning sounds as I fought to get some air.

My partner Doug was not enjoying this scene. The rope had jammed behind the piece that had held in the top part of the lower crack, a point 15 to 20 feet above his belay. He had felt very little when I hit the end of the rope. He had no control of the rope, as it was stuck above him. Try as he might, he could not get the rope to pull free. "Bummer," I thought, "I'm belayed by a stuck rope, and if it pulls there will be 25 feet of slack, and I'll fall to the ledges at the bottom of the first pitch and die." Terrific. I sat on a spike of rock and groaned and tried to clear my head. Doug gave me a few minutes to recover, and suggested that I climb up a few feet, giving him the slack to put me on a belay. Once on belay, I made it back to him after a few moves of 5.6. Those few moves jangled my three broken ribs, and from that point on every breath hurt more.

Rocky Mountain Rescue personnel were standing at the base of the climb by the time I struggled back to the belay. That's a pretty amazing response time. It couldn't have been more than 20 minutes from the time I fell to the time they showed up at the base of the route. I was embarrassed that I had caused all the ruckus, and that there would be another story in the paper about a climber falling. I have to admit that I was also embarrassed about falling off a "moderate" climb. Dumb ego, internal blather.

There was enough free rope to fix to the ground. The fall welded my tie-in knot, and we had to cut it free with a knife sent up by the Rocky Mountain Rescue people. (I may climb with a knife from now on.) Doug checked me out (he's a neurologist, I always take him along when I plan to get knocked out), lowered me off, and he and the RMR, took great care of me.

I appreciate Rocky Mountain Rescue and my partner Doug for their competence and quick thinking. After I was carried off, RMR people cleaned the gear off the climb and brought it to the hospital, including my Cebe sunglasses that fell 150 feet onto a granite slab and survived without a scratch. I'm healing nicely and can almost take a full breath now. I plan to be back to work next week and on the rock (or in the gym) in a month or so. I'm going to wear a helmet religiously now, and take more care in placing gear. The failure of the two upper pieces was my error, as the flake I had them in takes protection very well. I've been traditional climbing for ten years, and seldom have had a piece of protection fail me in a fall. Complacence, overconfidence, and carelessness may have played a role in this accident. Fortunately, you learn—if you happen to live through your errors. (Source: Robert Kooken)

FALLING ROCK—ROUTE OVERCROWDED, POOR POSITION
Colorado, Eldorado Canyon State Park, Red Garden Wall

On September 29, a climber (30) was recording the first pitch of Rewritten when a rock was knocked loose by a party higher up on the route. The rock struck and fractured her right forearm. (Source: J. W. Wilder, Park Ranger)

(Editor's Note: On the weekends in this park, it is typical to see 50 to 100 climbers in clusters of ten to twenty on the popular routes.)

FALL ON ROCK—RAPPEL ANCHOR SLING NOT TIED, DISTRACTION
Colorado, Aspen, Die Hard

On October 12, Jake McNelly (23) set up a rappel on a short sport climbing route at a popular cliff called Die Hard. McNelly had walked around to the top of the cliff to set up a top-rope above a half-pitch 5.8 route called Ain't Over 'Til It's Over. Two medium sized trees near the lip of the cliff typically are used for top rope anchors. According to the other climbers in the area, McNelly appeared to set his anchor and clip his rope into it, then tug on it before backing off the lip of the cliff, which forms a very clean, 90-degree break. At this point the climber began to free fall down the cliff. For most of the approximately 50-foot fall, he slid on his chest, ultimately landing on his right side at the base of the cliff and rolling approximately 20 feet downhill to stop at a tree.

The accident occurred about 1230. Other climbers rendered aid and were able to make a cell phone call for help within 15 minutes. Ambulance EMTs and an emergency room physician (also a member of Mountain Rescue-Aspen) were on the scene within 15 minutes of that call. An evacuation team arrived shortly thereafter. The victim, who was alert and oriented but inclined to perseverate (repeat himself), complained of back pain and difficulty breathing. He was placed on high-flow oxygen and intravenous fluids. He had no obvious deformities and showed good capillary refill. Spinal precautions were maintained to prevent further injury. He showed oxygen saturation rates of 90 percent or better and a heart rate of 90 during evacuation. The patient was littered 50 yards to the top of a scree slope, then lowered approximately 150 feet down the slope to an ambulance. The victim was loaded into the ambulance 30 minutes after the evac team arrived at the trailhead and 70 minutes after the first page was issued, departing the scene about 1430. The victim was continuing to complain of injuries at the time he was loaded into the ambulance.

McNelly was transported approximately ten miles to Aspen Valley Hospital, but died in the emergency room around 1530 of a ruptured aorta. Autopsy results suggested the aorta had been partially ruptured during the fall, developed a hematoma, and then ruptured fully. Also, there was noticeable bruising on the right temporal lobe, which could have led to the perseveration.

Analysis

Discussions with other climbers on the scene and inspection of McNelly's equipment suggest the following. First, McNelly set up a single rappel anchor, despite the fact that two anchors are located in close proximity. The sling used for this anchor reportedly fell to the bottom of the cliff with the climber, along with the single locking carabiner he had clipped in with, and his rappel device. Inspection of the sling revealed the following: three short sections of black, flat tubular webbing, tied together with water knots to form a sling about six feet long. Two single overhand knots were also present in the webbing, appearing by their tight configuration as if they had been left there for some time and been weighted. The sling was not tied. In each free end of the sling was the beginning of a loose water knot (the overhand tied before it is traced back with the second piece of sling), ruling out the possibility of a poorly tied knot pulling out. Rescuers concluded that McNelly wrapped the sling around the tree, started to tie the knot, became distracted, then started to tie it again with the other end of the sling, only to become distracted a second time. He then clipped in to the wrapped webbing and visually inspected it. A total of two full water knots and four half hitches were present in the webbing, making it possible that he looked at the sling and concluded that it was tied. When he tugged on it, the friction of the sling around the tree (which is about six inches in diameter, with low branches, making visual inspection difficult), could have confirmed his conclusion that the sling was tied. (Source: Mountain Rescue Aspen, Inc., compiled by Hal Clifford)

FALL ON ROCK, CLIMBING ALONE AND UNROPED
Colorado, Black Canyon of the Gunnison, Leisure Route
On October 19, Steven Permick (37), an experienced climber, was climbing alone in the Black Canyon. When he failed to return, his father called the Park Service. The body was spotted on a ledge halfway up the Leisure Route on Cruise Gully. Permick apparently was free soloing. At a crux move about 60 feet up the pitch, he may have been trying to place protection, but his rope was still in his pack. He fell about 60 feet and probably died soon after. (Source: Arden Anderson, Western State College Mountain Rescue Team)

FALL ON ROCK, INADEQUATE PROTECTION, NO HARD HAT
Connecticut, Ragged Mountain, Valhalla
There was a fatal accident on September 16 at the "Small Cliff" at Ragged Mountain in Connecticut. Following is the account of what I believe happened. At 1910, my climbing partner and I were walking down the Brierly's driveway on our way back to our car when we came across the belayer (whose name was John), who was visibly disturbed. We quizzed him and found that an accident had occurred. The leader had fallen about 40 feet from near the top of the cliff after running it out. He was alone at the base of the right end of the cliff, unconscious but breathing. John had just phoned the police from someone's house and was waiting to lead them up. We knew that the situation demanded our help so we grabbed a blanket from my car and sprinted to the Small Cliff. My partner stayed on the driveway at the shortest trailhead to the Small Cliff to show the rescue workers where to go and I ran to the victim.

It was obvious that the victim had sustained massive blows to the head. He had a weak pulse when I got there, but by the time the rescue workers arrived at the base of the cliff (probably five to ten minutes later), he did not. They performed CPR and evacuated him by ambulance and then helicopter. He did not survive.

Analysis
When I arrived, the victim (I believe his name was Paul) was face down at the base of the cliff. As near as I can tell, he had been leading a route called Valhalla (5.7) and had run it out to somewhere near the top of the cliff (50 feet in this area) before falling. Valhalla goes up about 15 feet to a large sloping ledge, then goes over a small overhang to a face with a thin crack to the top. He had very few pieces in (either three or four), and the

highest one was about half way up in the overhang. The rope was still attached to his harness when I arrived and there was nothing attached to it between the leader and the last piece of protection, so no pieces pulled. In addition, there was no protection in the crack above the last piece so it wasn't a case of a 'biner failing either. I'm not sure whether the leader fell and was initially stopped short of the ground (in which case he would have hit the large ledge) and then lowered, or whether he grounded out, but his knot was disturbingly easy to untie, suggesting that the rope had not held a great deal of force.

There are some lessons. Whatever led to this accident, my completely uneducated opinion is that he would have lived if he had been wearing a helmet. Certainly his head wounds would have been much less. Know the rock you are climbing on. These fellows had not done much climbing (if any) at Ragged. Leading on Traprock is VERY serious business. There is no fixed protection here and many of the routes demand subtle protection. A "G" protection rating may be conditional on your knowing or finding the one place where a particular brand and size of micro-nut fits. If you don't own that brand and size, it's "R" for you. In addition, the rock is soft and very fractured giving it the tendency to break when you least expect it. This may cause you to fall on easy terrain and cause your "bomber" protection to fail. I'm not sure I've ever backed off a Gunks route due to fear, but I've backed off many a Traprock route, as has almost everyone I know who climbs here. (Source: Lanier Benkard, Yale University)

FALL ON SNOW—UNABLE TO SELF-ARREST, CLIMBING UNROPED, INADEQUATE BOOTS AND CRAMPONS, INEXPERIENCE
Montana, Glacier National Park, Mount Jackson

On January 8, Kyle Borchert (20), Shad O'Neel (22) and Taggart Schubert (25) obtained a five-day backcountry permit for a winter trip into the Lake Ellen Wilson area, via the Sperry Trail, of Glacier National Park. They completed the voluntary climber registration for climbing Mount Jackson and listed Borchert as the leader and their experience as "novice." They departed the same day and reached about 4.5 miles up the Sperry Trail where they camped.

They continued on the next day and reached Lincoln Pass where they spent the next two days pinned down by a storm, the first night in a tent and the next night in a snow cave. On the 11th they moved on to Lake Ellen Wilson where they established "base camp" for climbing in the area. The weather had improved considerably by this time.

They decided to attempt the summit of Mount Jackson (3,064 meters) and at 0630 on the 12th began their ascent, equipped with technical climbing equipment and extensive bivouac gear. Borchert and O'Neel were wearing heavy climbing boots with 12-point crampons, while Schubert was wearing heavy pack boots with 4-point instep crampons. Each had an ice ax. Their ascent generally followed the Gunsight Pass route directly up from the pass. Because of terrain and high wind encountered, they remained roped and protected the ascent using snow pickets all the way to the summit.

They reached the summit about 1445 and immediately began their descent via the Northeast Ridge route due to extreme wind conditions. They decided to unrope a short distance below the summit to move faster. The wind was pulling on the rope and continually throwing them off balance. The slope angle seemed to ease up and each believed they could self-arrest if needed.

They descended approximately 600 meters to a point above several cliff bands with Borchert and O'Neel route-finding about 50 meters ahead of Schubert. Borchert and

O'Neel were stopped at the top of the cliff bands, discussing route alternatives, when they heard Schubert fall above them, then saw him slide past in a self-arrest position. Schubert was unable to arrest his slide before falling over the first cliff band, estimated to be about 15 meters high. Schubert continued sliding down a steep snowfield separating the cliff bands, appearing flaccid and no longer attempting to self-arrest. Schubert then slid over another cliff band, estimated to be about five meters high, and onto the main snowfield where he continued sliding out of control for about 120 meters before coming to a stop.

Borchert and O'Neel descended rapidly to Schubert and found him to be alive but in grave condition. Schubert had suffered a fractured femur and was having difficulty breathing (later determined to be multiple fractured ribs on both sides).

Borchert and O'Neel dug a snow trench and made Schubert as comfortable as possible. O'Neel departed at 1530 to get help. Borchert stayed with Schubert trying to shelter and keep Schubert warm, an effort which proved difficult in their exposed position, continuous high winds, drifting snow and sub-zero temperatures. Schubert's condition steadily deteriorated through the night. About 0230, he succumbed to his injuries and the cold.

With remarkable effort, O'Neel made it all the way out and reached a phone just after midnight on the 13th and notified Park Rangers of the situation. A first-light helicopter response, with ALS and technical rescue equipment, was organized and dispatched to the scene. In extremely marginal flying conditions, Borchert was rescued from the scene, where he was suffering initial stages of hypothermia and frostnip to his hands and feet. Schubert's body was then recovered.

Analysis

The actual cause of the accident remains a mystery. The start of Schubert's fatal slide was not witnessed. Contributing factors may have included Schubert's footwear used on wind slab and ice. While Schubert was not reported as having any difficulty during descent, the cumulative effects of fatigue, extreme cold and wind, haste, and dehydration may have contributed to diminished attention and caution at the initial, fateful moment. Schubert's inability to self arrest within the first 50 meters could be attributed to the steep, hard slab conditions and/or to lack of experience and training, rendering his efforts ineffective. Schubert was not wearing a climbing helmet but, incredibly, received only superficial head injuries in the incident.

While the climbers had some experience in winter mountaineering, none had ever attempted a winter ascent on a major peak. They had borrowed much of the technical equipment they carried and reported minimal training and experience in technical application. Schubert was the least experienced. (Source: Charlie Logan, SAR Coordinator, Glacier National Park)

FALL ON ROCK, PLACED INADEQUATE PROTECTION, PROTECTION PULLED OUT, NO HARD HAT, MISCOMMUNICATION
Nevada, Juniper Canyon, Red Rocks

On November 11, three climbers were ascending Olive Oil (5.7), a seven pitch route in Juniper Canyon and were on the last pitch when the belayer told the leader (46) that there was only ten feet of rope left. Shortly thereafter, the leader called, "Off belay." About 20 minutes passed without any communication between her and her partners.

Two other parties came to the ledge, both guided. One guide climbed up to see what the delay might be. He found the leader hanging upside down, about 30 feet below a piece of protection. She had obvious head injuries and was unconscious. Both guides then climbed to her and lowered her to the ledge on top of the fifth pitch. One of them then went for help.

The Las Vegas Metropolitan Police Department helicopter was dispatched, and rescue personnel got to the ledge to establish a lowering system. They found that the victim had succumbed. She had sustained a massive basilar skull injury.

Analysis
The victim had been climbing for ten years, but had just started leading this year. She was described as able to follow 5.10, but had limited leading experience. The guidebook advises taking large gear to protect the last two pitches. She may not have had adequate gear to protect, though since the guides took her rack, we have no idea what she had. That she was not wearing a helmet obviously led to her fatal injury.

Request: If you come across an accident like this, don't remove gear if at all possible. Leave it for the SAR team. Removing evidence from the scene makes analysis very difficult. (Source: Russell Peterson, SAR Officer, LVMPD)

(*Editor's Note: Peterson reported three other accidents from the area, but they were hikers who had gone astray. One of them, a 32 year old male with a church group, had gone "scrambling" in the cliffs above their picnic area. He was last seen traversing on a small, exposed rock ledge high above. He fell 200 feet, striking the rocks three times before landing at the bottom, fatally injured. This kind of event often gets identified as a "climbing" accident, which for our purposes it clearly is not.*)

AVALANCHE, FAILURE TO FOLLOW DIRECTIONS—WARNING NOTICES, INEXPERIENCE
New Hampshire, Mount Washington, Lion Head Trail
On January 5, the body of Alexandre Cassan—one of four members in a party attempting an ill-advised winter ascent of the 6,288-foot peak—was discovered by a U. S. Forest Service snow ranger about one hour after the 1420 avalanche near the Lion Head Trail on Mount Washington's steep southeast slope. All but one hand of Cassan was buried in the snow. The French Canadian hiker and his three companions apparently lost their way while attempting to climb up the recently closed Lion Head winter hiking trail. After losing the trail a short distance from its start off the popular Tuckerman Ravine Trail, the group made its way into an area that is prone to snow avalanches. Authorities are unsure if the hikers created the avalanche themselves, or if they just happened to be in its path. Cassan was discovered in an area just a couple of hundred feet from where rescuer Albert Dow was killed in a similar avalanche 14 winters ago.

U. S. Forest Service snow ranger Brad Ray said warning signs alerting hikers to the high avalanche danger were posted at the base of the mountain at the Appalachian Mountain Club's Pinkham Notch Visitor Center, and along the trail. Additionally, signs warning hikers that the old Lion Head Trail had been closed permanently were also in place. Forest service snow rangers Chris Joosen and Brad Ray both responded to the scene immediately. Joosen was first to arrive and he spotted Cassan's hand sticking out of the snow-covered slope.

Analysis
The French-speaking Quebec hikers, who had some winter hiking experience, may have misunderstood the warning signs, said Rebecca Oreskes, a public information specialist for the U. S. Forest Service. Nonetheless, the hikers had been advised by AMC personnel in the area not to attempt the hike up the mountain as conditions on the summit were extreme—with minus 33 degree temperatures and 100 mile per hour winds—and the avalanche danger on the mountain's lower slopes very high.

The Lion Head winter trail, long a favorite of winter climbers on Mount Washington, was closed by the Forest Service two months ago after a late autumn landslide created increased winter avalanche risks along the route. Last month the Forest Service established a new alternate route up the mountain. This new route, while steeper than the Lion Head winter trail, is signed and open for winter hiking use. (Source: From an article by Mike Dickerman in *The Courier*, Littleton, NH, January 10, 1996)

(Editor's Note: Had Cassan's partners done a hasty search before going for help, they might have seen his hand. This was one of six deaths in the Presidential Range, four of which would be classified as skiing- and hiking-related incidents. Two were skiing on Gulf of Slides when another skier triggered an avalanche, and they were in the path of it.

Two other fatalities were the result of falling. In one case, a man on top of Lion Head rocks dropped his sun glasses, and when he went to recover them, he fell into Tuckerman Ravine. The other case was a climber who took off his rope on easy ground near the top of Pinnacle Gully and went to see other climbers. He fell to his death, just missing two other solo climbers.

The sixth victim died from exposure and hypothermia during his descent from Mount Eisenhower on a cold winter day.)

FAULTY USE OF CRAMPONS—GLISSADING
New Hampshire, Frankenstein Cliff and Gulf of Slides
At Frankenstein a woman was doing a seated glissade from just below Standard Route She caught a crampon and was flipped face down for the remainder of the slide to the trucks. Her ankle was injured and she had to be carried to the parking lot.

In the Gulf of Slides a man was doing a seated glissade when he caught a crampon. He flipped and impaled himself on his ice ax through his mid-section. He walked out to the AMC Pinkham Notch Camp with the ax still through his abdomen from the upper left to lower right quadrant. No organs were injured.

Analysis
There is no good reason for glissading with sharp spikes on our feet. (Source: George Hurley)

FALL ON ROCK, INADEQUATE PROTECTION
New Hampshire, Cathedral Ledge, Book of Solemnity
On August 15, a husband and wife team were climbing The Book of Solemnity on Cathedral. The leader crossed the crux traverse (5.9+) in the second lead without placing protection. He belayed at the end of the traverse at the trees on Upper Refuse. The second climber fell while trying to make the hard moves at the crux. Since the rope ran

nearly horizontally to her left, she swung down and left into the wall, sustaining a very bloody compound dislocation and fracture of her left ankle.

Analysis
How can this kind of accident be prevented? First, a leader could continue the lead until he is directly above the crux. This option would require a leader on The Book to climb the 5.5 third pitch of Upper Refuse without placing protection. Using double ropes (the UIAA wants us to call this "half-rope technique") and clipping only one rope after the crux would allow both leader and follower to have protection. Second, a leader could place protection on the traverse. On The Book, a small Tricam or SLCD fits in a downward opening slot in the middle of the crux.

What could a second climber do when she gets to the start of a dangerous and unprotected traverse? She could leave in the last two (or more) pieces of protection before the traverse and ask to be lowered. On The Book, a 50 meter rope would put her back on the tree-covered ledge. Second, she could leave her rope through the highest protection (adding pieces if she doubts their safety), fasten one end of a quick-draw to her harness and the other end to the rope above (beyond) the protection, and ask the leader to slowly lower her across the traverse. Or, if she is dragging a haul line she could use the haul line, running from her harness through the protection and back to a belay device on her harness, to lower herself across the traverse. The second will end up well below the leader which is OK if there is climbable rock or if she knows how to prussik. If the leader did the lowering, the second will need a place to stand (or hang from a prussik) while she ties a figure-of-eight on a bight on the strand of rope going up to the leader. After she clips this knot to her harness with a locking carabiner (or with two opposed ordinary 'biners), she can untie her original tie-in knot and pull the tail of the rope through the gear which she happily deserts. Another option does not abandon gear, but is more complicated. Ask. (Source: George Hurley)

FALL ON ROCK, INADEQUATE PROTECTION, PROTECTION PULLED OUT, EXCEEDING ABILITIES
New Mexico, Sandia Mountains, Muralla Grande
On June 23, Carlos Abad (26), Jane Tennessen (33), and Glen Tietgen (35), fell 816 feet from Muralla Grande, a massive face of granite east of Albuquerque. They were ascending a route called Warpy Moople (III, 5.9), a climb with eight pitches. The route is clean, with solid crack and face climbing.

After the party failed to return home, search and rescue teams were dispatched. They found the climbers at the base of the wall, and proceeded with an investigation.

Analysis
Based on careful examination of the route, the equipment left behind and the damage it sustained, the following is a possible scenario.

Carlos Abad leads the last pitch (5.6) and tops out. Jane Tennesen goes off belay, undoes her anchor, and begins climbing, with Glen Tietgen putting her on belay from below. Abad then falls from the top, zippering out the stopper he had placed and putting a major impact on a Friend, which umbrellas out. The force of his fall pulls his partners with him.

While the total story will never be known, one of the messages is to place adequate protection—more than you think you should. (Source: Marc Beverly and Steve Attaway, Albuquerque Mountain Rescue)

VARIOUS FALLS ON ROCK and INADEQUATE PROTECTION, and ONE HORNET ATTACK
New York, Mohonk Preserve, Shawangunks
Of the 18 incidents reported form the Shawangunks in 1996, twelve were the result of leader falls, with six of those exacerbated by inadequate protection. Sixteen accidents occurred while ascending, one of them being a 160-foot fatal fall while soloing. There was only one report of a falling rock/object, and that happened to a rappeller, though we don't know how the rock was dislodged from above. There were six cases resulting in fractures, while the rest resulted in sprains, lacerations, or abrasions. There was only one report of stings, but it was a very serious one, because the victim is "deathly allergic" to bee stings. In this case, they were white faced hornets encountered at the end of the first pitch of Le Teton (5.9). Thaedra (23) worked quickly to set some protection, because she knew that if (more likely when) she passed out, she could fall 70 feet to the deck. Her epi-pen, unfortunately, was in her pack on the ground below. Her partner came to the rescue, part of which could be called an epi-epic, as he climbed up to her unroped with epi-pen in mouth! He too was stung—about 15 times—before getting the epi-pen to her and effecting a lower. A trip to the hospital that included another shot and some benadryll led to a sufficient recovery.

There was a case of rope being used on rope, resulting in a sling being worn through while lowering. A thirty foot fall resulted in a fracture and concussion. The average age of victims was 30, and the only climb of any difficulty was a 5.10, from which the leader (48) fell within the first six feet.

One full report, sent in to ANAM by the climbers, follows below. (Source: From the report submitted by Mohonk Preserve and Jed Williamson)

FALL ON ROCK, INEXPERIENCE
New York, Shawangunks, Shockley's Ceiling
On September 6, 1996, Robyn Williams (19) and I—Sean Hartman (21)—were climbing the classic climb Shockley's Ceiling (5.6) at the Gunks. I had been climbing for about six months, and Robyn had taken a NOLS course which involved climbing and had done some climbing on her own, but not much in the way of multi-pitch. The third pitch has the ceiling about 20-30 feet above the belay ledge. After the ceiling, the route climbs a left-facing corner, traverses out to the right around the edge of the corner, and continues to the top. Communication is very difficult between the top and the belay ledge; simple communications are possible (e.g., "On belay," etc...), but anything more just sounds like garbled shouts. I reached the top, set up an anchor, and put Robyn on belay. She fell several times attempting the roof. Each time, by feel, I lowered her back to the ledge to start over. (Falling as a follower on Shockley's leaves you hanging away from the rock.) She managed to move over on the ledge to a point where we could actually talk; she said she was going to climb to the left of the ceiling and traverse back to the corner. I told her it was okay if she "felt safe" doing it. She said she did, and succeeded in placing herself

in a position horizontal to the next piece of protection (about 15 feet up the corner over the roof), but still eight feet to the side of it, when she fell. She pendulumed hard into the corner, badly bruising her left ankle and opening a deep laceration to her left knee. (I didn't know she was hurt.) This occurred around 1230. I also did not know that the sheath of the rope (a single 10.5) broke right above her tie-in knot, although the core remained fully intact. Not knowing where she was at this point, I left her hanging for a little while, hoping she could get back on the rock. Soon thereafter I lowered her back to the ledge. We were unable to communicate in a meaningful manner at this point. When I shouted down, "Are you okay?" I got back, "Yeah," and then some garbled shouts; she was trying to tell me she wasn't seriously injured, but couldn't really climb.

To make a long story short, it was two hours (around 1430) before I tied her off to get help. (Those two hours were spent waiting and trying to communicate.) Help came in the form of a climbing instructor who was climbing with his son a few climbs over from us. We wound up rappelling, administering first aid (both he and Robyn were WFR's) and lowering her off in a couple of pitches while I went to get the ranger. Robyn was carried from the base of the climb down to the ranger truck a couple of hundred feet over rocky terrain in a litter with the help of a couple of climbers who were in the area. We were back to our cars around 1600 or 1630.

Analysis
Robyn actually had several full-length runners with her, which would have allowed her to prussik over the roof. She apparently did not know that she could use these to ascend the rope. Although she did know the prussik knot, she had forgotten her usual prussiking cord at home that morning. A couple of points came up in retrospective analysis of this incident:

(1) If I had any doubt as to Robyn's ability on the climb, I either should not have done it or set up a belay right after the roof to help coach her over.

(2) I should have made sure she had the proper prussiking materials with her and knew how to use them.

(3) After being lowered to the ledge, Robyn should have reestablished the anchor and clipped into it (especially given the condition of the rope), but she did not.

(4) The lowering and rappelling that ensued, from what Robyn told me, took place from less than solid anchors.

(5) She does not recall banging her head. We were both wearing helmets, which I think is always a good idea.

(Editor's Note: What is implied here is that these two climbers did not know each other—at least not very well in terms of climbing. Picking up partners at climbing areas like this is quite commonly done. Often, as in this case, not enough information is communicated.)

FALL ON ROCK, INADEQUATE PROTECTION—ANCHOR SLING KNOT
North Carolina, Stone Mountain, The Great Arch
On May 25, I was climbing at Stone Mountain, NC. Hoping to do some sport climbing (I read that the routes were sparsely bolted) I brought only a limited rack. I climbed the first pitch on the entrance to "The Great Arch" and prepared to set up a top-rope so that my wife could enjoy a climb. I tied a sling (nylon webbing) to a tree and had my wife lower me off. About halfway down it became apparent that my rope was too short. I

climbed back to the top and found a lower tree to girth hitch the sling to. When I leaned back to lower off, the water knot on the sling popped open. I fell 30 feet before snagging a bush, still 60 feet off the ground. During the fall, my ankle snagged in the crack and broke in two places. Some of the local climbers set up a rope which enabled a guy to rap down to me, tie me into his harness, and then rap the rest of the way down the crag.

This accident has "impatient" and "unprepared" written all over it. Because most of my one year prior climbing experience took place in a gym, my concept of climbing had little to do with safety. I mistakenly thought that if I could physically do a climb, then all would be well. Solid anchoring systems was something prior to that accident I simply hadn't given much thought. The impatient part came about due to an approaching thunderstorm. I wanted to get that climb in before the storm came and "ruined" my chance to climb.

The guys that got me off the bush—which I'm sure saved my life—were excellent, and I am extremely grateful to them. I hope I can return the favor.

I'm sending this in because a friend of mine read an accident report that sounded exactly like mine (one sling, water knot pops, broken ankle, guys from NC to the rescue) except it took place in Joshua Tree. The similarity is amazing. Also, I hope people will learn more about safety before moving from the gym to the crags. (Source: David Tart)

FALL ON ROCK, EXCEEDING ABILITIES, NO HARD HAT
North Carolina, Whitesides Mountain, New Diversions

Labor Day was the date that my climbing partner, Todd (29), and I (41) had set to finally climb Whitesides Mountain. About a month's worth of planning had gone into our climb. We had selected the route, New Diversions (5.10), and were looking forward to our first bivvy.

I had been climbing almost weekly for about four years while Todd had been actively climbing about two years longer. I am a 5.8 leader with a couple 5.10 top rope and sport climb successes while Todd leads 5.10 with a few 5.11 climbs under his harness. ("Way-honed hardmen" is not a climbing accolade either of us will be hearing any time soon.) Neither of us had ever taken a serious lead climbing fall.

As we made the 3½ hour drive from Charlotte to Cashiers, we wondered if the article in the (then) current issue of *Climbing* magazine along with the mild weather and holiday weekend would make Whitesides more like "Woodstock" with hordes of wannabe big-wall climbers (like us) crowding the mountain.

But when we reached the parking lot at the tourist trail there were only two other cars there. Each party was pretending to be asleep, thinking we might be rangers there to enforce the "no camping" policy. Our late-night preparations for the following morning "awakened" the other parties and they, too, began racking gear and checking route descriptions. Fortunately, the others had designs on routes other than the one we had in mind.

The route book said the first pitch was a runout 5.7, so I was surprised to find a good #0 Camalot placement only 20 feet up. With the possibility of hitting the deck minimized, I continued on to the first belay with no problem. Mentally confirming the moderate grade, I felt reassured that this would be no sandbag epic.

Todd led pitch two, another 5.7 section only better protected. After pulling the haul bag up, I followed. Two or three moves up I spied a nicely shaped flake to pull on. "Great hold!" I thought. As the little flake snapped off, my normally "cat-like" reflexes could do nothing as I watched the pancake-sized rock smack me squarely between the eyes. As I shook off the cobwebs, I wondered two things: What would have happened had I been leading? and Would a helmet have deflected the blow, had I been wearing one? (Neither Todd nor I owned a helmet.)

The rest of the pitch went easily and after pulling up the haul bag a second time we felt we could reach the sixth pitch bivvy well within the allotted time frame. I led pitch three (silently thankful that it would be Todd's turn to pull the haul bag this time) placing gear liberally to protect the climb. Near the end of the pitch I came to a small roof section. After scanning the line for the best means of ascent (read, "path of least resistance"), I decided to place extra gear to back up the horn I had girth-hitched as my primary point of protection. Feeling confident in my gear (if not my alleged abilities) I committed to the small roof. Once into the sequence I found that the moves that looked so reasonable from ten feet away now seemed several grades harder. Frantically trying to remain calm, I quickly checked all the available handholds and footholds. Seconds later I was at the "moment of decision" when I knew I would have to commit to a sequence of moves or completely pump out and fall. My feet were on good rock, though I was on tiptoe. The most reasonable looking handhold was up and to the left, barely within reach. I reached for it and realized immediately it was a sloper with no edge to prevent my fingertips from sliding off.

My next conscious thought was, "Wow! My gear held!" As I pendulumed high above the ground, I tried to remain calm but the rush of adrenaline made me giddy. Todd yelled up, asking if I was all right. I was pumped and out of breath, but realizing that my gear was intact I responded, "Yeah—just give me a few minutes and I think I can do this." As I collected my thoughts hanging off the rock face, I did a mental and physical inventory. The only apparent damage was some slight skin abrasion to both of my exposed ankles.

Ten minutes later, my heart rate still elevated (read, "scared shitless"), I began to feel pain in both my ankles. I relayed this information down to Todd and after some discussion we decided that I would rappel down the belay and he would lead the section. When I reached the belay, both ankles were swelling. Todd led the pitch back to the point of my fall and made it through with the comment, "Yeah, that section's kinda tough." He set up the belay and I began climbing.

Weighting my ankles with climbing moves produced serious pain in both ankles. No stranger to sports injuries, I had the sinking feeling that this was not the kind of pain that would be going away soon. When I reached the point of my fall I knew I would not be able to weight my ankles enough to do the crux moves. I pulled out my ascenders and fixed them to the rope. As I was adjusting the lower one, I dropped it. I had the presence of mind to yell, "ROCK," as I watched my beloved gear bounce 200 feet to the base of the mountain. Insult had been added to injury.

At the belay we took stock of our situation. My ankles were looking worse by the moment. I felt responsible for screwing up our climb and voted to bivvy on the ledge we were resting on for the night. Todd voted for aborting our climb and rapping off the mountain. When the effects of the adrenaline still pumping through me wore off, I might not be able to limp out by morning, he argued.

After an hour's rest we began to rappel the three pitches to the base. My ankles were swollen twice their normal size and I began to believe I had broken both. Forty-five excruciating minutes later we were at the base of the mountain with about a hundred pounds of gear, darkness descending, and an hour hike back to my van. (An hour hike for a healthy individual, that is.) Todd was gracious enough to carry 75 pounds of the gear and promised to come back for me after loading it in my van. I estimated that it would take me four hours to make it back. Three hours later, having crawled on my hands and knees and fashioned a crutch of sorts from a tree branch for pitiful limping, I saw Todd's headlamp on the trail ahead. He relieved me of the rest of the gear and I promised to meet him at the van. An hour and a half later I crawled down the stairs leading to the parking area and back to my van where an equally exhausted Todd lay sleeping. It was 0030.

My wife, awakened by my noisy entrance at 0430, came downstairs fearing someone was breaking in. Quite shocked by my presence, she (a nurse) quickly confirmed my diagnosis: two severely sprained ankles. It turned out my situation was not that bad. I crawled around on my hands and knees for the remaining two days of my long weekend holiday and ate large quantities of ibuprofen to minimize the pain. By the fifth or sixth week following my accident I went climbing again, but was only able to climb sub-5.7 routes. Not only had I lost significant strength, my alleged "boldness" was decimated as well.

Now, almost five months after my accident, I am finally climbing at my former level. I am hoping to convince Todd to attempt New Diversions again next Labor Day. I think I'll wear a helmet this time. (Source: Wayne Brown)

(Editor's Note: All due respects, Mr. Brown, but I think wearing a helmet isn't the only thing to consider on your next try at this climb.)

FALL ON ROCK, CLIMBING ALONE AND UNROPED
Oregon, Smith Rock State Park, Monkey Face Spire

On May 22, Terry Mitchell (22) a Willamette University student and climbing instructor, set out to free-climb, without the aid of ropes or safety devices. With him were two other experienced climbers, Mike W. Heald (22), also an instructor, and Miri Marie Anderson.

They'd climbed the rock before, and their experience had given them the confidence to try the route without ropes, said deputy Neil Mackey, search and rescue coordinator for Deschutes County.

Heald went first, making his way up a route called Monkey Face Spire, to a ledge. Mitchell went next. A little more than halfway to the top, Mitchell fell 500 feet to the ground and died. It was unclear whether he slipped or whether a handhold or foothold crumbled, searchers said. A climber from another party witnessed the accident at 1100 Saturday and called 911 with a cellular telephone.

Analysis
Mitchell reportedly climbed here almost every weekend and usually used ropes and protection. (Source: From an article in the *Oregonian*, May 27, 1996)

FALL ON ROCK, INADEQUATE PROTECTION
Oregon, Columbia River Gorge, Broughton Bluff

On May 28, Kurt Gierlich (42) fell 60 feet to the ground from a route on Broughton Bluff. Someone with a portable phone called 911, and a rescue followed. Twelve rescuers spent an hour lowering him 500 feet to a point where a Life Flight helicopter could pick him up.

He suffered multiple fractures and internal injuries. (Source: From a report in the *Oregonian*, May 28, 1996)

(Editor's Note: Gierlich was wearing a harness and rope, but there was no indication how he fell or what his partner was doing. It is interesting to note that Tom Layton, a chief in Fire District 14, said, "This is a real common occurrence. We pull about five or six climbers out of here every year.")

STRANDED, FAILURE TO FOLLOW ROUTE, CLIMBING ALONE AND UNROPED, HASTE, WEATHER
Oregon, Mount Hood

On Friday, May 31, I arrived at Timberline Lodge at 2330 with the intent of climbing Mount Hood via the Sandy Glacier Headwall, a moderate snow and ice route. I hiked to the summit via the south side/Hogsback route before sunrise. Finding excellent snow conditions and clear, cold weather, I headed to the Sandy Glacier. Once on the Sandy Glacier, I made the critical error of failing to traverse far enough to the west. This left me at the base of the Sandy Couloir route rather than the Sandy Glacier Headwall route. I climbed the couloir to its top, where I was shocked to find rime-covered rock towers where I expected low angle snow slopes leading to the summit. I realized my error and recognized the rock towers were the upper buttress of the Yocum Ridge. It was late morning by this time and the ambient temperature had risen dramatically. I tried to climb east into the Leuthold Couloir, but was impeded by difficult rock climbing. My attempts to traverse west onto the Sandy Glacier Headwall and to downclimb the Sandy Couloir were stymied by deteriorating snow conditions. I planned on waiting until the next morning for the snow to consolidate before making another attempt at downclimbing the route. I alerted a climbing party on the Reid Glacier to my predicament in case I would not be able to extricate myself.

This, indeed, became the case as the night was warm and snow conditions failed to improve. I waited Sunday for my eventual rescue which came in the form of an Air Force helicopter.

Analysis

I was climbing very fast, intending to summit twice in one day. I simply made a careless route finding error. Because I was attempting an easy route, I relaxed, got caught up in the fantastic climbing and made a stupid mistake. Climbing, especially alpine solo climbing, is a game in which constant vigilance is necessary. Had I been paying attention, this incident could easily have been avoided. (Source: Daniel Smith-27).

(Rescuer's Note: Although this mission resulted in a successful air evacuation, the Air Force rescue helicopters [MH-60 Pavehawks] made two attempts before the extrication. The very warm temperatures which created the unstable snowpack and rendered the ground approach unsafe, also created density-altitude limitations for the aircraft. Mountaineers should be aware that rescue helicopters may be limited, despite "fair weather" conditions at even moderate altitudes. Getting off route on the approach to this particular route has happened before, and often enough so that it has prompted a warning in the guidebook. (Source: Jeff Sheetz, Portland Mountain Rescue)

(Editor's Note: There was another Oregon report of one fatality on Mount Thielson involving a young woman (20) who left her hiking partner to continue "a little farther" on more technical terrain. Her partner stopped, and shortly thereafter, she saw the fall. Kristen Gehling landed on her head after a 20 foot fall, then slid another 200 feet in the loose shale. Whether this was an intended technical climb or not, the terrain turned from a hiking venture into a climbing event.)

FALLING ROCK
Washington, Guye Peak

On June 1, while climbing on the lower part of the south section of Guye Peak's West Face, Kristin Beerli was struck and injured by a large (about 100 pounds) rock slab that came loose while she was being top belayed. Seattle Mountain Rescue personnel responded, and a MAST helicopter from Fort Lewis was dispatched. The victim was rescued and transported to a medical center where she was treated for a punctured lung.

During the rescue, the medic's pack was blown off the ridge by rotor downdraft. It tumbled 300 feet down the face, scattering the contents over the scree slope below. Observers reported that the helicopter rotor had contacted tree branches while hovering above the victim. (Source: *Bergtrage*, Number 148, December 1996)

RAPPEL ANCHOR FAILURE, INADEQUATE PROTECTION, FALL ON ROCK
Washington, Mount Thompson

On September 17, John Cain and Dale Ramquist climbed Mount Thompson via the West Ridge. Instead of going down the East Ridge, the normal descent route, they opted to descend by rappelling their ascent route. They reportedly had a disagreement about the quality of their first rappel anchor, and, over Cain's objections, Ramquist proceeded to rappel. The anchor apparently failed as soon as he loaded it, precipitating a fall down the northwest corner and out of sight of Cain, taking both ropes in the process. Cain hiked out for help, presuming Ramquist had been killed in the fall.

Seattle Mountain Rescue personnel (first five, then three more) and Guardian I responded to the scene. At 0830 on the 18th, Ramquist was spotted by Guardian I. He waved. MAST's Blackhawk helicopter arrived and the victim was extricated.

It was later learned that Ramquist's injuries were minor, including a cut on his left leg and lots of bruising. In fact, he was ambulatory, in spite of an estimated 50 to 60 foot fall.

Analysis

Single point rappel anchors need to be bombproof. The type of anchor these two had set up is not known, other than the fact that it was not adequate. (Source: *Bergtrage*, Number 148, December 1996)

(Editor's Note: Reports were not submitted in time for publication from the key areas in Washington—Mount Rainier, Olympic, and North Cascades National Parks. They will be included next year.)

FALL ON ROCK, PROTECTION PULLED OUT, INADEQUATE PROTECTION
West Virginia, Seneca Rocks, Prune

John Markwell, owner of the Gendarme Climbing Shop at Seneca Rocks, reported that there had only been one severe accident there this year. On the second pitch of Prune, there is a stance just below a finger crack, where most climbers place protection, and then two or three moves above. If climbers can place protection above these moves, they are generally in good shape in the event of a fall. The victim's belayer was able to stop him three feet from the ground after an 80-90 foot screamer. However, John reports that this spot on Prune claims an injury almost every year.

Last year, there was a fatality, and this year a climber suffered a broken arm, fractured skull, and knee damage. He fell just above the ledge and pulled out all of his protection on the way down. (Source: Jim Yester)

FALL ON ROCK, CLIMBING UNROPED
Wisconsin, Devil's Lake State Park

On June 21, two young men (18 and 19) were climbing without ropes in a remote area of the park when one of them dislodged a rock and started to fall. The rock then struck the second climber, causing him to fall. The first victim fell about 80 feet, the second about 20 feet. Injuries were several and significant. The second victim was able to crawl to a dry creek bed and spent the night there. The next morning, he was spotted near the Badger Army Ammunition Plant by a guard. Both subjects were then extricated and taken by ambulance to the local hospital. (Source: Steven Schmelzer, Park Ranger)

(Editor's note: There were four other incidents reported from Devil's Lake. Three were falls while leading, and one was a 15 year old on a top rope who fell and pendulumed, resulting in a broken arm. Ranger Schmelzer reported that his rough estimate is that there are about 15,000 climbers who visit this park annually. On busy days they have 300 or more climbers on the bluffs.)

RAPPEL ERROR—ROPE JAMMED, STRANDED, OFF ROUTE
Wyoming, Grand Tetons, Black Ice Couloir

On July 6, while ascending the Grand Teton around 0800, Park volunteers Lanny Johnson, PA, and Dr. Jim Little heard several loud whistles and distress calls emanating from the Black Ice Couloir at the top of the Upper Saddle. Johnson immediately notified the Jenny Lake Rangers by radio and began to investigate the incident.

Given the seriousness of the location and the lack of availability of contract helicopters (which were out of the valley on fires), all available personnel were summoned to the rescue. About 1000, the Eastern Idaho Regional Medical Center (EIRMC) helicopter became available and was dispatched to Grand Teton National Park.

Johnson interviewed several concerned climbers in the area and was finally able to communicate verbally with the involved party. At 1020, Johnson ascertained that party members Larsen Inman and Sam Parsons had no injuries. However, they had become stranded on a ledge in the Great West Chimney about 200 feet below the level of the Upper Saddle the previous day, and were quite cold and exhausted. At 1100, Rangers

Randy Benham and Bill Culbreath were delivered to the Lower Saddle by the EIMRC helicopter. Four additional rangers were prepared to fly to the Lower Saddle as well, but the EIMRC helicopter was called back to its base in Idaho for dispatch to another medical emergency.

Benham and Culbreath, along with Johnson and Little, then solicited the assistance of two Exum Climbing Guides, Jim Olsen and Ken Jern, who were also in the area guiding clients. Rangers Leo Larson and Chris Harder were dispatched on foot from the valley to the Lower Saddle to assist in the operation. Rangers Helen Larson and Scott Guenther were situated in Cascade Canyon at a convenient location to assist with communications.

At 1400, Culbreath was lowered 200 feet to the stranded climbers. Inman was secured to a rope and raised to a ledge connecting to the Upper Saddle using a Z-rig pulley system. The operation was repeated for Parsons and Culbreath. At 1645 all personnel arrived at the Upper Saddle. Inman and Parsons were then escorted by rescue personnel to the Lower Saddle and arrived at 1800. Being quite exhausted, they opted to spend an additional night at their camp on the Middle Teton Moraine, 500 feet below the Lower Saddle.

Analysis

While descending the Grand Teton in the late afternoon, Inman and Parsons had become disoriented. Instead of rappelling down the "normal" route, which ends at the Upper Saddle, they ventured too far to the north, and rappelled into the Great West Chimney of the Grand Teton. When they attempted to pull their rope down to them to continue their descent, the rope became jammed. They were subsequently forced to spend the night at the location since they were unable to contact any other climbers until the next morning. (Source: George Montopoli, Park Ranger)

FALL ON ROCK—HAND HOLD CAME OFF, INADEQUATE PROTECTION, OFF ROUTE
Wyoming, Grant Tetons, Symmetry Spire

On July 14, Chris Schroeder (34) and his partner Ronald Fleck were attempting an ascent of the Southwest Ridge of Symmetry Spire (II 5.7). Schroeder was leading the second pitch and believes that he was off the regular route. He had placed a small spring loaded camming unit and proceeded to "run it out" on easy climbing when he pulled out a loose rock. This caused him to fall approximately 70 feet before the rope halted his fall approximately five feet above a ledge. Schroeder remembers bouncing off a ledge and injuring his left ankle. He then began to tumble and in the process cut his left hand. He believes he would have landed on the ledge if his belayer had not taken in slack and shortened his fall. Schroeder was not wearing a helmet at the time of the fall.

Following the incident Fleck treated his injuries and then lowered Schroeder a rope length to the ground. He had a cellular phone with him but was unable to phone out on it until they were near the trail. Once at the base of the climb, Fleck continued lowering his partner down the snow couloir as much as possible. Schroeder was also able to "scoot" himself down the slope unassisted at times. Schroeder stated that he had been doing roped climbing for approximately 15 years. (Source: Rich Perch, SAR Ranger)

SLIP ON SNOW, UNABLE TO SELF-ARREST, INEXPERIENCE
Wyoming, Grand Tetons, Middle Teton

Around 1700 on August 1 in the South Fork of Garnet Canyon, Carrissa Johnson (18) was injured when she slipped on snow while descending from the Southwest Couloir of the Middle Teton. She was with a party of nine other Coulter Bay employees, some of whom had camped at the Platforms on the night of July 31. They left the Platforms about 1000 on the morning of August 1 and arrived on the summit of the Middle Teton around 1500. The group had talked about the use of ice axes, but Johnson had not done any actual practice.

Several of the party descended a snowfield into the South Fork without incident. Johnson glissaded part of the way down the snowfield, then lost control and rolled about 100 feet to the rocks below. She hit the rocks with her back and bounced to a lower ledge.

Brandon Osterman reached Johnson in a few seconds and began checking her condition. She had not lost consciousness and could feel and move her extremities. At 1800 Johnson was helped to the camp of some climbers about a quarter of a mile down canyon from the accident site. One of the group, Stewart Harman, and the occupants of the camp stayed with Johnson during the night. David Albano descended to the valley for help.

At 2145 a climber from a separate group, who had seen the accident from a distance, called Grand Teton dispatch, who contacted the SAR coordinator, Tom Kimbrough. Another passing climber who did some medical assessment reported to Kimbrough at 2240. This assessment indicated a possibility of a back injury and possible internal injuries. After consultation with medical coordinator Lanny Johnson, a decision was made to dispatch two climbing rangers to evaluate Johnson's condition. Rangers Jim Phillips and Andy Byerly started up at 2400 with medical equipment. David Albano reported in with more information at 0030.

By 0600 on the morning of August 2, Phillips and Byerly were searching the South Fork of Garnet without result. While they descended to the Platforms to see if Johnson had reached that point, Rangers Leo Larson and Bill Culbreath climbed the Middle Teton from the Lower Saddle and descended the Southwest Couloir into the South Fork in search of Johnson. Larson and Culbreath located Johnson at 0830.

The Yellowstone LAMA arrived at Lupine Meadows at 0945 and began airlifting equipment and rescuers into Garnet. By 1045 Rangers Alexander, Benham, Wise and Yellowstone Ranger Steve Underwood were assisting Phillips, Byerly, Culbreath and Larson in lowering Johnson to the helicopter landing site. The lowering was complete by 1200 and Johnson was flown to Lupine Meadows, accompanied by Phillips, arriving at 1220. She was taken to St. John's Hospital by ambulance where she was treated for cuts, bruises and abrasions and released. (Source: Tom Kimbrough, SAR Ranger)

(Editor's Note: While the frequency of summer employees getting into situations like this has decreased, there are still one or two major incidents each year. Those who are working for concessions in the park receive a fairly thorough briefing—but they do not always engage in the training that is suggested.)

FALL ON SNOW—CRAMPON POINT CAUGHT IN PANTS, NO HARD HAT, CLIMBING ALONE
Wyoming, Mount Owen, Koven Couloir

At 1300 on August 2, Randy Huskinson (46) was descending the Koven Couloir following a successful ascent of the East Ridge of Mount Owen. He had soloed the route and was alone when he fell approximately 500 feet on snow to the base of the couloir.

Huskinson sustained multiple injuries in the fall and was unable to move unaided. Mark Savage and Clay Roscoe were climbing in the area and discovered the injured climber around 1400. They treated his injuries and sent other climbers in the area for assistance from Grand Teton National Park rangers. Six rangers from the Jenny Lake Rescue Team were flown to the accident site in the evening and climbed to the patient with medical and rescue gear at 2012. The rescue team along with Savage and Roscoe stabilized him and lowered him a short distance to a ledge where they could spend the night. On August 3, at 0845, the contract helicopter from Bridger-Teton National Forest conducted a "short-haul" of Huskinson to the landing zone on Teton Glacier. He was then transported in the helicopter to the rescue cache at Lupine Meadows and then by NPS ambulance to St. John's Hospital in Jackson.

Huskinson had sustained a C-7 vertebrae fracture, bilateral second rib fractures, multiple lacerations, penetrating knee injury, and various soft tissue injuries.

Analysis

Huskinson had left Lupine Meadows Trailhead around 0500 on August 2 for a solo day climb of Mount Owen. His partner for the climb had not shown up as planned, so he opted to do the climb alone. He ascended the East Ridge route and reached the summit about 1100. The descent was uneventful until 1300, approximately halfway down the Koven Couloir where the angle began to lessen. He had been front pointing down the shaded portion of the couloir. The route now was exposed to the direct sunlight and the snow conditions were changed. Huskinson stamped out a small platform in the snow to evaluate whether to remove crampons and/or face out for the remainder of the descent. The step he had created in the snow collapsed and he took several plunge steps down the slope in order to regain control. One of his crampons caught on his pant leg which caused him to fall head first down the snow slope. He managed to work his body into a self-arrest position and was nearly stopped when he hit a rock and lost his ice ax. Huskinson slid head first again down the slope, hitting rocks along the way and eventually stopped on a small ledge. He believes that he did not lose consciousness, but he was unable to move himself from his location. He attempted to stop the bleeding from his scalp wound through direct pressure. Huskinson owns a helmet but had neglected to bring it with him on the climb. He stated that he had been climbing for 15 years, mostly in the Teton range. He had climbed the Koven Route previously. (Source: Rich Perch, SAR Ranger)

STRANDED, PARTY SEPARATED—OFF ROUTE, LATE START, INEXPERIENCE
Wyoming, Grand Tetons, Grand Teton

On August 14 at 2230, rangers at the Lower Saddle hut were contacted by Chris Riha (39), Rosa Kanning (24), and John Murphy (23) who indicated that two of their party, Jason Osder (22) and Margaret Knight (22), were lost.

At 0400 Osder, Knight, Murphy and Kanning had left the Lupine Meadows trailhead for the camping zone in Garnet Canyon. The party arrived at the Meadows about 0800 and set up their camp. They then continued up to the Lower Saddle, arriving at 1210. The party intended to climb the Owen-Spalding (OS) route on the Grand Teton, and arrived at the Upper Saddle at 1500. At this point they joined with a solo climber, Riha, who offered to lead the party to the summit. The party of five climbed the OS, and summitted at 1800. On the descent, the party reached the Upper Saddle, via the normal rappel, at 2015.

At this time, Osder and Knight, both novice climbers, decided to get a head start on the descent to the Lower Saddle. They were told to stay near the central rib on the way down, and to avoid the gully closest to the west face of the Grand. Osder and Knight apparently became lost in the growing darkness, and descended the Exum gully. They continued to a point at which they were cliffed out, and with only one headlamp between them and the now total darkness, they sat down to be found.

Riha, Kanning, and Murphy descended toward the Lower Saddle. As they were passing through the Black Dike area, they heard cries for help from their stranded friends. They attempted to make clear voice contact with Osder and Knight, but were unable to determine their exact location. After approximately one and a half hours of searching, they decided to continue to the Lower Saddle to get help.

At 2230 Riha, Murphy, and Kanning arrived at the Lower Saddle Hut. Rangers Wilts, Arial, and Guenther went up with Murphy to search for the lost party. They ascended toward the start of the Lower Exum route and were able to make minimal voice contact. Rangers Arial and Guenther then ascended the normal approach route for the Upper Exum climb and began descending the Exum Gully. Contact was made about 0100. Osder and Knight were both uninjured and found to be alert and oriented.

Rangers Arial and Guenther then proceeded with roped belays to assist Osder and Knight back up the gully and then down the standard descent route. The entire party reached the Lower Saddle at 0430. All five members of the climbing party stayed at the Exum Hut on the Lower Saddle until about 1000 that morning. (Source: Mark Magnusen, SAR Coordinator)

Analysis

There is no explanation as to why Riha offered to suddenly become a guide—or what his level of experience was. Having taken on some responsibility for these novices, he should have followed one of the basic principles: keep the party together. (Source: Jed Williamson)

SNOW BRIDGE COLLAPSE, UNROPED
Wyoming, Wind River Range, Gannett Peak

On August 16, about 1420, Bob Farley and his partner Tony were descending the Gooseneck route of Gannett Peak when the snow bridge leading from the upper snowfields of the route onto the Gooseneck Glacier collapsed under Bob's weight. He fell nearly 30 feet into the bergschrund, and was trapped there by the snow bridge debris. Tony was able to leap across the crack and dig out his partner, who was disoriented, sore along most of his left side, and had a deep laceration on his face. Tony stopped the bleeding and cared for Bob's injuries. Around 1700, under Tony's guidance, the two descended a short distance to bivouac for the night. At first light of August 17, the two descended the rest of the Gooseneck Glacier, where Tony left Bob at 0730 to enlist the help of our party camped at the base of the route. Though at first Tony was eager to use a radio to call for help, with some assistance he and Bob were able to return to their camp on the far side of Dinwoody Pass. With their two companions they continued from there to the roadhead, 18 miles away, several days later.

Analysis

Bob and Tony were climbing a route that had received much travel in the preceding days, and they followed a well-worn trail up to and across the snow bridge. However, many days of hot conditions had substantially weakened the bridge, and by the time Bob and Tony descended, it was ready to collapse. A short belay over this gaping bergschrund, with the rope that they carried, probably would have prevented Bob's fall and saved them a cold night on the mountain. It is all too easy to assume that because you are following the tracks of other climbers that you are out of harm's way; in fact, eliminating your own decision-making process from your climbing makes you a more likely candidate for an accident.

Once Tony and Bob found themselves in trouble, however, they proved themselves well equipped to deal with the situation, and responded well. They carried a first aid kit that was adequate to care for Bob's facial lacerations, and enough layers to bivvy—though they were fortunate to have a calm, clear night. In the morning, Tony roped up with Bob for the remainder of the glacier and rock descent, and safely assisted him to a low point on the mountain. It is worth noting that to Tony the situation seemed serious enough to warrant a radio call when he left Bob to find us in the morning, but that after a survey of Bob's injuries this was deemed unnecessary. Food, water, and friendly faces greatly reduced the apparent severity of their situation. In the end, despite their fatigue, Bob and Tony were able to walk, with assistance, over the pass that separated them from their camp and waiting companions. After a rest day, they continued out of the mountains on their own. We were happy to be able to provide the perspective and manpower to avoid a time-consuming and costly rescue effort. (Source: Richard Morse, NOLS Instructor)

Further comments from the victim: I landed nearly head first and was almost completely buried but for part of one leg. Tony saved my life by making me an air hole and then spending the next 45 minutes digging me out. I had a concussion and a large gash on my left temple. We had no choice but to spend the freezing night on the mountain.

The next day we began the climb down the mountain with the thought of having to ascend up Bonny Pass and down to our camp at Titcomb Basin where our friends and my day-old fiancee were waiting and wondering what had made us so late. On the way down we ran into three young climbers who told us of a NOLS group camped at the base of the glacier. Tony left me in a safe spot and went to them for help. And help they did.

NOLS leaders Ian and Richard, along with four of their students, rushed to us like the cavalry. They tended to my injuries, fed and hydrated both of us, and helped us over the pass. It was hard enough with their help; without them it would have felt impossible. Please tell Richard, Ian and all the NOLS students who helped us, thanks.

I had sustained a concussion, at least four broken ribs (I'm still waiting on the results of a CAT scan and a bone scan), and a rather large gash. Thanks to Richard and Ian, that is healing nicely. I'm going to have a scar to help me remember that mountains teach hard lessons. Doctor Johnson in Pinedale approved of their handiwork. Pass along a thank you to Richard, Ian and all the students. Again, thanks for all the assistance. (Source: Bob Farley)

FALL ON SNOW, UNABLE TO SELF-ARREST
Wyoming, Grand Tetons, Middle Teton

On August 20 around 1400, while descending the Southwest Couloir of the Middle Teton, Paul Schladensky (34) fell on a snowfield just above the Middle/South Teton Saddle. He initially attempted to arrest using only his hands and heels (while on his buttocks). After a while he tried to use his ice ax. He was unable to arrest and slid about 100 feet on snow into talus, hitting his right hip, chest, and ribs on the rocks first. He did not lose consciousness, but experienced difficulty with breathing, and was unable to continue on his own due to the soreness and pain, especially in the back.

Matthew Rusher, Schladensky's partner, provided him with additional clothing and water, and went for help. He contacted campers in the South Fork of Garnet Canyon. Two of the campers continued below in search of help, while Rusher and two other campers returned to the accident site. In the Garnet Meadows, the campers contacted Forrest McCarthy, Exum guide, who cell-phoned Jenny Lake Rescue about 1530. A rescue operation was then initiated.

At 1445 Ranger Lanny Johnson, who is also a Physician's Assistant, was informed. At 1610, the Bridger-Teton Long Ranger helicopter arrived at Lupine Meadows Rescue Cache. After a briefing, Rangers A. Byerly and R. Johnson were flown to the area for an initial evaluation and landed at the knoll just above and to the north of the saddle. Four additional rangers were flown to the same landing zone.

After informing medical control about the patient's status, a shorthaul evacuation to a lower landing site was suggested by L. Johnson and supported by all involved rescue personnel. About 1800, the shorthaul litter and other equipment were long-lined to the accident site, and the helicopter landed at the lower landing zone while the patient was packaged for shorthaul. Shortly afterwards, the helicopter returned to the site and shorthauled the patient to the lower landing zone, where he was then loaded into the helicopter. The patient was flown to St. John's Hospital, arriving at 1920.

Schladensky was diagnosed with five broken ribs, a fracture/dislocation of the third sacral vertebrae, a hemo/pneumothorax, a pulmonary contusion, and several abrasions and lacerations. He was later flown to St. Vincent's Hospital in Billings, Montana. (Source: George Montopoli, SAR Ranger)

(Editor's Note: This was one of the seven incidents that happened as a result of a slip or fall on snow. Five of these victims—four females, one male—were inexperienced. This is an unusually high number of "unable to self-arrest" cases. But it was also a year when the snow pack was considerably above normal.

Additional incidents in the Grand Tetons include two leader falls on The Snag in Death Canyon that resulted in fractures, and one Ichabod Crane-like sighting. The latter was a report from a climber on the summit of Teewinot around noon on September 7. Looking at the North Ridge route on the Grand through binoculars, he thought he saw a rope and a body hanging on the end in a belly-up position, with arms and legs dangling. He watched for 30 minutes, and was "80% sure" it was a body. A fairly thorough investigation did not turn up any evidence to substantiate the report. When this kind of imagery occurs— especially when one is awake and alert—one should consider trying a different sport for awhile.)

ROCK DISLODGED—CAUSING FALL ON ROCK
Wyoming, Devil's Tower National Monument

On August 20 at 1445, Jeff Pettenger (21) was leading a variation of the Bailey Direct finish to the Durrance Route when he fell approximately 100 feet, receiving fatal head injuries. Jeff's father, Noel Pettenger, summoned help from other climbers. Immediate assistance was provided by Markus Silpala and Jim McDermott, who climbed up to the

Pettengers. McDermott, a paramedic, attempted to secure and maintain an unobstructed airway. However, Jeff Pettenger's breathing eventually slowed, then stopped; and his heart subsequently stopped a short time later. Further attempts at basic life support were not attempted due to the injuries, location and evacuation considerations. Jeff Pettenger was recovered by the Devil's Tower Search and Rescue Team. He was pronounced dead at the base of the Bowling Alley by Physician's Assistant Bob Cummings at 1840. (Source: Jim Schlinkman, NPS Ranger)

Analysis
At 0930 on August 21, Robert Moelder and I ascended the fixed lines left the evening before to the ledge that was the scene of the Pettenger fatality.

There we found the equipment left behind from the previous day. We completed the route via the Jump Traverse and gained the summit.

From the summit we rappelled down, over the pitch from which J. Pettenger had fallen. Here we photographed the climbing gear as placed by Jeff the day before. We observed a fresh rock scar, indicating that a rock had recently fallen, about 12 feet below the belay ledge at the end of the pitch.

The route J. Pettenger chose as the last pitch to their route is one crack right of the Bailey Direct route. This pitch is 112 feet long. Twelve feet from the finish we observed a 24" x 24" mark on the face of a column indicating that a rock had recently dislodged. Fifty feet lower we found the highest piece of climbing gear placed in the crack. Four other pieces of climbing gear were found placed in the crack between the highest piece and the ledge Jeff Pettenger landed on. All distances are approximate. (Source, Chris Holbeck, NPS Ranger)

(Editor's Note: Chief Ranger Jim Schlinkmann estimates from registrations that about 5000 climbers visited the Tower during the year.)

TABLE I
REPORTED MOUNTAINEERING ACCIDENTS

	Number of Accidents Reported		Total Persons Involved		Injured		Fatalities	
	USA	CAN	USA	CAN	USA	CAN	USA	CAN
1951	15		22		11		3	
1952	31		35		17		13	
1953	24		27		12		12	
1954	31		41		31		8	
1955	34		39		28		6	
1956	46		72		54		13	
1957	45		53		28		18	
1958	32		39		23		11	
1959	42	2	56	2	31	0	19	2
1960	47	4	64	12	37	8	19	4
1961	49	9	61	14	45	10	14	4
1962	71	1	90	1	64	0	19	1
1963	68	11	79	12	47	10	19	2
1964	53	11	65	16	44	10	14	3
1965	72	0	90	0	59	0	21	0
1966	67	7	80	9	52	6	16	3
1967	74	10	110	14	63	7	33	5
1968	70	13	87	19	43	12	27	5
1969	94	11	125	17	66	9	29	2
1970	129	11	174	11	88	5	15	5
1971	110	17	138	29	76	11	31	7
1972	141	29	184	42	98	17	49	13
1973	108	6	131	6	85	4	36	2
1974	96	7	177	50	75	1	26	5
1975	78	7	158	22	66	8	19	2
1976	137	16	303	31	210	9	53	6
1977	121	30	277	49	106	21	32	11
1978	118	17	221	19	85	6	42	10
1979	100	36	137	54	83	17	40	19
1980	191	29	295	85	124	26	33	8
1981	97	43	223	119	80	39	39	6
1982	140	48	305	126	120	43	24	14
1983	187	29	442	76	169	26	37	7
1984	182	26	459	63	174	15	26	6
1985	195	27	403	62	190	22	17	3
1986	203	31	406	80	182	25	37	14
1987	192	25	377	79	140	23	32	9
1988	156	18	288	44	155	18	24	4
1989	141	18	272	36	124	11	17	9
1990	136	25	245	50	125	24	24	4
1991	169	20	302	66	147	11	18	6
1992	175	17	351	45	144	11	43	6
1993	132	27	274	50	121	17	21	14
1994	158	25	335	58	131	25	27	5
1995	168	24	353	50	134	18	37	7
1996	139		261		100		31	
Totals	4656	677	8388	1492	3954	535	1127	235

TABLE II

| | 1951–1995 | | | 1996 | | |
Geographical Districts	Number of Accidents	Deaths	Total Persons Involved	Number of Accidents	Deaths	Total Persons Involved
Canada						
Alberta	338	103	730			
British Columbia	251	97	546			
Yukon Territory	33	26	73			
Ontario	31	8	58			
Quebec	25	5	54			
East Arctic	7	2	20			
West Arctic	1	1	2			
Practice Cliffs[1]	13	2	18			
United States						
Alaska	355	143	525	20	7	35
Arizona, Nevada Texas	57	9	106	2	2	5
Atlantic–North	656	96	1107	29	4	51
Atlantic–South	63	15	100	2	0	4
California	914	226	1911	29	7	61
Central	106	10	174	6	1	11
Colorado/Oklahoma	569	174	970	23	3	45
Montana, Idaho South Dakota	60	22	93	2	1	2
Oregon	128	60	313	4	2	6
Utah, New Mexico	109	34	195	1	3	3
Washington	892	266	1591	3	0	6
Wyoming	434	99	795	18	1	32

[1]This category includes bouldering, as well as artificial climbing walls, buildings, and so forth. These are also added to the count of each state and province, but not to the total count, though that error has been made in previous years.

(Editor's Note: The Practice Cliffs category has been removed from the U.S. data and replaced with Artificial Walls.)

TABLE III

	1951–95 USA	1959–95 CAN.	1996 USA	1996 CAN.
Terrain				
Rock	3369	398	95	
Snow	2000	297	38	
Ice	180	84	2	
River	12	3	1	
Unknown	22	6	0	
Ascent or Descent				
Ascent	2969	422	91	
Descent	1843	286	48	
Unknown[3]	247	3	0	
Immediate Cause				
Fall or slip on rock	2324	212	68	
Slip on snow or ice	754	152	20	
Falling rock, ice or object	467	105	12	
Exceeding abilities	381	27	18	
Avalanche	249	105	4	
Exposure	231	12	3	
Illness[1]	255	20	14	
Stranded	249	48	9	
Rappel Failure/Error	188	33	8	
Loss of control/glissade	164	15	2	
Fall into crevasse/moat	125	38	4	
Failure to follow route	113	20	8	
Piton pulled out	84	12	0	
Nut/chock pulled out	88	3	9	
Faulty use of crampons	60	5	5	
Lightning	39	6	0	
Skiing	45	9	3	
Ascending too fast	43	0	0	
Equipment failure	7	2	0	
Other[2]	166	18	15	
Unknown[3]	59	8	0	
Contributory Causes				
Climbing unroped	875	143	14	
Exceeding abilities	819	154	9	
Inadequate equipment/clothing	531	68	10	
Placed no/inadequate protection	417	51	46	
Weather	362	46	7	
Climbing alone	307	53	9	
No hard hat	216	22	11	
Nut/chock pulled out	160	16	9	
Darkness	110	15	4	
Party separated	95	16	2	
Piton pulled out	82	10	0	

	1951–95 USA	1959–95 CAN.	1996 USA	1996 CAN.
Contributory Causes (cont.)				
Poor position	103	13	4	
Inadequate belay	100	18	7	
Failure to test holds	65	18	1	
Exposure	54	10	1	
Failed to follow directions	56	5	4	
Illness[1]	32	4	0	
Equipment failure	9	4	0	
Other[2]	220	79	7	
Age of Individuals				
Under 15	112	11	0	
15-20	1123	196	19	
21-25	1392	222	30	
26-30	995	186	28	
31-35	654	93	15	
36-50	800	105	24	
Over 50	124	18	4	
Unknown	836	466	52	
Experience Level				
None/Little	1440	269	31	
Moderate (1 to 3 years)	1303	334	29	
Experienced	1286	350	50	
Unknown	1375	241	62	
Month of Year				
January	173	12	5	
February	175	37	2	
March	236	44	82	
April	320	28	8	
May	683	43	22	
June	804	51	26	
July	895	209	16	
August	811	119	29	
September	1035	46	13	
October	323	29	12	
November	149	5	3	
December	60	16	1	
Unknown	4	0	0	
Type of Injury/Illness (Data since 1984)				
Fracture	633	120	58	
Laceration	332	46	32	
Abrasion	182	37	21	
Bruise	208	50	16	
Sprain/strain	165	18	13	
Concussion	109	12	6	
Frostbite	76	6	1	
Hypothermia	83	10	14	

	1951–95 USA	1959–95 CAN.	1996 USA	1996 CAN.
Type of Injury/Illness (cont.)				
Dislocation	64	6	3	
Puncture	25	4	2	
Acute Mountain Sickness	14	0	3	
HAPE	47	0	2	
HACE	14	0	2	
Other[1]	173	27	10	
None	82	31	21	

[1]These included: AMS (3), HAPE, HACE (2), exhaustion (4), frostbite, appendicitis, twisted/strained back, allergic reaction—bees, hemo/pneumothorax, punctured lung, slight hangover.
[2]These included: multiple stings, distraction, unable to self-arrest (5), inadequate food (2), inadequate fuel, failure to turn back (3), bolt broke when loaded, route selected had extreme objective dangers (2), unable to extricate—crevasse, rope jammed—rappel device, late start, haste (3), carabiner broke (loaded with gate open), carabiner lock gate jammed shut, miscommunication, psychological (2), misperception: rappelled into deep pool—unable to ascend rope (drowned—exhaustion/hypothermia), dead cell phone battery.

(Editor's Note: Under the "other" category, many of the particular items will have been recorded under a general category. For example, the climber who fell into his unanchored partner knocking him off would be coded as Fall on Rock, Falling Rock/Object, and Placed Inadequate Protection. The point in this category is to provide the reader with some added detail. It should be apparent that many of these details can be translated into a few basic categories.)

MOUNTAIN RESCUE ASSOCIATION OFFICERS

Tim Cochrane, *President*
PO Box 115
Vail, CO 81658

Tim Kovacs, *Vice President*
PO Box 4004
Phoenix, AZ 85030

John Wehbring, *Secretary/Treasurer*
4980 Pacific Drive
San Diego, CA 92109

Don Adamski, *Member at large*
6734 W. Multnomah Blvd.
Portland, OR 97223

Jon Inskeep, *Member at large*
5224 Bubbling Well Lane
La Canada, CA 91011

MOUNTAIN RESCUE ASSOCIATION, INC.
200 Union Boulevard, Suite 430-1355
Denver, CO 80220

MOUNTAIN RESCUE GROUPS IN NORTH AMERICA
(Where not obvious, area covered is indicated in parentheses)
*Indicates membership in Mountain Rescue Association

ALASKA
Alaska Mountain Rescue Group,* PO Box 241102, Anchorage, AK 99524
U. S. Army Northern Warfare Training Center,* Fort Greeley, AK, APO Seattle 98733
Denali National Park Ranger Station, Talkeetna, AK 99676

ALBERTA
Banff Park Warden Service, Banff National Park, PO Box 900, Banff, Alberta T0L 0C0
Jasper Park Warden Service, Jasper National Park, PO Box 10, Jasper, Alberta T0E 1E0
Kananaskis Park Warden Service, Kananaskis Provincial Park, General Delivery,
    Seebe, Alberta T0L 1X0 (Alberta outside National Parks)
Waterton Park Warden Service, Waterton National Park, Waterton, Alberta T0K 2M0

ARIZONA
Arizona Mountaineering Club Rescue Team, PO Box 1695, Phoenix, AZ 85030
Central Arizona Mountain Rescue Association,* PO Box 4004, Phoenix, AZ 85030
Grand Canyon National Park Rescue Team,* PO Box 129, Grand Canyon, AZ 86023
Southern Arizona Rescue Association, Inc.,* PO Box 12892, Tucson, AZ 85732
Sedona Fire Dept./Technical Rescue Group, PO Box 3964, West Sedona, AZ 86340

BRITISH COLUMBIA
Columbia Mountain Rescue Group, Royal Canadian Mounted Police, Invermere,
B.C. V0A 1K0 (East Kootenays)
Glacier Revelstoke Park Warden Service, Glacier Revelstoke National Park, PO Box
    350, Revelstoke, B.C. V0E 2S0)
Kootenay Park Warden Service, Kootenay National Park, PO Box 220, Radium Hot
    Springs, B.C. V0A 1M0
Mountain Rescue Group, c/o Frank Baumann, PO Box 1846, Squamish, B.C. V0N
    3G0 (Coast Range, Northern Cascades)
North Shore Rescue Team,* 165 East 13th Street, North Vancouver, B.C. V7L 2L3
YoHo National Park Warden Service, Box 99, Field, B.C., Canada V0A 1 GO

CALIFORNIA
Altadena Mountain Rescue Team, Inc.,* 780 E. Altadena Drive, Altadena, CA 91001
    (Los Angeles County)
Bay Area Mountain Rescue Unit, Inc.,* PO Box 6384, Stanford, CA 94309 (Northern
    Sierra Nevada)
China Lake Mountain Rescue Group,* PO Box 2037, Ridgecrest, CA 93555 (Southern
    Sierra Nevada)
De Anza Rescue Unit, PO Box 1599, El Centro, CA 92243 (Imperial Valley, Baja)
Inyo County Sheriff's Posse,* PO Box 982, Bishop, CA 93514
Joshua Tree National Monument SAR,* 74485 National Monument Dr., Twenty-nine
    Palms, CA 92277
June Lake Mountain Rescue Team,* P. O. Box 436, June Lake, CA 93529

Los Padres Search and Rescue Team,° PO Box 30400, Santa Barbara, CA 93130
Malibu Mountain Rescue Team,° PO Box 222, Malibu, CA 90265
Montrose Search and Rescue Team,° PO Box 404, Montrose, CA 91021
 (Los Angeles County)
Riverside Mountain Rescue Unit,° PO Box 5444, Riverside, CA 92517
 (Riverside County)
Saddleback Search & Rescue Team, PO Box 5222, Orange, CA 92667
San Diego Mountain Rescue Team,° PO Box 81602, San Diego, CA 92138
San Dimas Mountain Rescue Team,° PO Box 35, San Dimas, CA 91733
San Gorgonio Search & Rescue Team, San Bernardino Sheriff, San Bernardino,
 CA 92400 (San Bernardino Mountains)
Santa Clarita Valley Search and Rescue,° 23740 Magic Mountain Parkway, Valencia,
 CA 91355
Sequoia-Kings Canyon National Park Rescue Team,° Three Rivers, CA 93271
Sierra Madre Search and Rescue Team,° PO Box 24, Sierra Madre, CA 91025
 (Southwestern United States, Baja, California)
Yosemite National Park Rescue Team, Inc.° PO Box 577, Yosemite National Park,
 CA 95389

COLORADO
Alpine Rescue Team, Inc.° PO Box 934, Evergreen, CO 80439 (Front Range)
Colorado Ground Search and Rescue,° 2391 S. Ash Street, Denver, CO 80222
Crested Butte Search and Rescue,° PO Box 485, Crested Butte, CO 81224
El Paso County Search & Rescue, Inc.,° PO Box 9922, Manitou Springs, CO 80932
Eldorado Canyon State Park,° PO Box B, Eldorado Springs, CO 80025
Garfield Search & Rescue,° PO Box 1116, Glenwood Springs, CO 81602
Grand County Search & Rescue,° PO Box 172, Winter Park, CO 80482
Larimer County Search & Rescue,° PO Box 1271, Fort Collins, CO 80522
Mountain Rescue—Aspen, Inc.° PO Box 4446, Aspen, CO 81612 (Western Slope)
Ouray Mountain Rescue Team, PO Box 220, Ouray, CO 81427 (Gunnison National
 Park, Rio Grande National Forest, Uncompahgre Park)
Rocky Mountain National Park Rescue Team,° Estes Park, CO 80517
Rocky Mountain Rescue Group, Inc.,° PO Box Y, Boulder, CO 80306
San Juan Mountain SAR, PO Box 4, Silverton, CO 81433
Summit County Rescue Group,° PO Box 1794, Breckenridge, CO 80424
Vail Mountain Rescue Group,° PO Box 115, Vail, CO 81658
Western State Mountain Rescue Team,° Western State College, Gunnison, CO 81231

IDAHO
Idaho Mountain Search and Rescue,° PO Box 8714, Boise, ID 83707
Palouse-Clearwater Search and Rescue,° Route 1, Box 103-B, Troy, ID 83871

MAINE
Baxter State Park Mountain Rescue Team,° 64 Balsam Drive, Millinocket, ME 04462

MONTANA
Glacier National Park, SAR Coordinator, West Glacier, MT 59936
Lewis and Clark Search and Rescue,° PO Box 473, Helena, MT 59601

NEW HAMPSHIRE
Appalachian Mountain Club, Pinkham Notch Camp, Gorham, NH 03581 (White
    Mountains)
Mountain Rescue Service,° PO Box 494, North Conway, NH 03860

NEW MEXICO
Albuquerque Mountain Rescue Council,° PO Box 53396, Albuquerque, NM 87153
St. John's College Search and Rescue Team, 1160 Camino de Cruz Blanca, Santa Fe,
    NM 87501 (Northern New Mexico, Southern Colorado)

NORTHWEST TERRITORIES
Auyuittuq Park Warden Service, Auyuittuq National Park, Pangnirtung, N.W.T.
    X0A 0R0
Ellesmere Island Warden Service, Ellesmere Island National Park and Reserve,
P.O. Box 353, Pangnirtung, NT, XOA ORO

OREGON
Alpinees, Inc.,° 3571 Belmont Dr., Hood River, OR 97301 (Hood River County)
Corvallis Mountain Rescue Unit,° PO Box 116, Corvallis, OR 97339 (Central
    Cascades)
Crater Lake National Park Rescue Team, PO Box 7, Crater Lake, OR 97604
Eugene Mountain Rescue,° PO Box 10081, Eugene, OR 97401 (Oregon Cascades)
Hood River Crag Rates,° 1450 Nunamaker, Salem, OR 97031
Portland Mountain Rescue,° PO Box 1222, Portland, OR 97207

UTAH
American Search Dogs,° 4939 Benlomand, Ogden, UT 84003
Rocky Mountain Rescue Dogs,° 9624 S. 1210 E., Sandy, UT 84070
Salt Lake County Sheriff Search and Rescue,° 2942 Cardiff Road, Salt Lake
    City, UT 84121
Zion National Park°, Chief Ranger, Springdale, UT 84767

VERMONT
Mountain Cold Weather Rescue Team, Norwich University, Northfield, VT 05663
Stowe Rescue Squad, Stowe, VT 05672

VIRGINIA
Appalachian Search and Rescue Conference°, PO Box 430, Flint Hill, VA 22627
    (Blue Ridge and Shenandoah Mountains and Southwest Virginia)

WASHINGTON
Bellingham Mountain Rescue Council°, PO Box 292, Bellingham, WA 98225
    (Whatcom County)
Central Washington Mountain Rescue Council°, PO Box 2663, Yakima, WA 98907
    (Washington)
Everett Mountain Rescue Unit°, PO Box 2566, Everett, WA 98203 (North Central
    Cascades)

Mount Rainier National Park Rescue Team*, Longmire, WA 98397 (Mount Rainier National Park)

Seattle Mountain Rescue*, PO Box 67, Seattle, WA 98111 (Washington)

North Cascades National Park Rescue Team*, 2105 Highway 20, Sedro Woolley, WA 98284

Olympic Mountain Rescue*, PO Box 4244, Bremerton, WA 98312 (Olympic Range, Cascades)

Olympic National Park Rescue Team*, 600 Park Ave., Port Angeles, WA 98362 (Olympic National Park)

Skagit Mountain Rescue Unit*, 128 4th St., Mount Vernon, WA 98273 (Northern Cascades)

Tacoma Mountain Rescue Unit*, 7910 "A" St., Tacoma, WA 98408 (Central Washington, Cascades, Olympics)

WEST VIRGINIA
Gendarme/Seneca Rocks Climbing School, PO Box 23, Seneca Rocks, WV 26884

WYOMING
Grand Teton National Park Mountain Search and Rescue Team*, PO Box 67, Moose, WY 83012 (Grand Teton National Park)

Mountain Rescue Outing Club, University of Wyoming, Laramie, WY 82071 (Wyoming)

YUKON
Kluane Park Warden Service, Kluane National Park, Haines Junction, Yukon Y0B 1L0